FEMINIST FIELDWORK
ANALYSIS

SHERRYL KLEINMAN

Qualitative Research Methods
Volume 51

SAGE Publications
Los Angeles · London · New Delhi · Singapore

For information:

Sage Publications, Inc.
2455 Teller Road
Thousand Oaks,
    California 91320
E-mail: order@sagepub.com

Sage Publications India Pvt. Ltd.
B 1/I 1 Mohan Cooperative
    Industrial Area
Mathura Road, New Delhi 110 044
India

Sage Publications Ltd.
1 Oliver's Yard
55 City Road
London EC1Y 1SP
United Kingdom

Sage Publications Asia-Pacific Pte. Ltd.
33 Pekin Street #02-01
Far East Square
Singapore 048763

Printed in the United States of America

Library of Congress Cataloging-in-Publication Data

Kleinman, Sherryl.
Feminist fieldwork analysis / Sherryl Kleinman.
    p. cm.— (Qualitative research methods; v. 51)
Includes bibliographical references and index.
ISBN 978-1-4129-0549-7 (pbk.)
    1. Social sciences—Field work. 2. Sociology—Field work.
3. Feminist theory. 4. Sexism. 5. Equality. I. Title.

H62.K586 2007
300.72—dc22   2006034728

Printed on acid-free paper.

07   08   09   10   11   10   9   8   7   6   5   4   3   2   1

Acquiring Editor:	Lisa Cuevas Shaw
Editorial Assistant:	Karen Margrethe Greene
Production Editor:	Sarah K. Quesenberry
Copy Editor:	Rachel Keith
Proofreader:	Andrea Martin
Indexer:	Ellen Slavitz
Typesetter:	C&M Digitals (P) Ltd.
Marketing Manager:	Stephanie Adams

CONTENTS

1-88   9/20

ACKNOWLEDGMENTS

I came to feminism by reading authors I've never met and talking to people I have been lucky enough to know. The bibliography of this book provides a list of many of the works that influenced my fieldwork and thinking. When I was preparing to teach my first course in Race, Class, and Gender, I came across the writings of Marilyn Frye, Sandra Bartky, Alison Jaggar, and bell hooks. These authors (among others) helped me not only teach, but finish a fieldwork project that had been lingering.

For feminist conversations, insights, humor, and emotional support over the years, I thank Karen Booth, Martha Copp, Elyse Crystall, Jessica Fields, and Martha McMahon. Matt Ezzell and Krista McQueeney read parts of the manuscript and offered helpful comments and strong encouragement. John Van Maanen, one of the editors of this series, sent me more comments than I wanted to handle, but the manuscript is immeasurably improved because of them. I am thankful for his close reading. Current and former graduate students in my fieldwork classes and other seminars, including Stacey Cutbush, Marianne Cutler, Natalia Deeb-Sossa, Heather Kane, and Ken Kolb, provided motivation and support.

Michael Schwalbe and I talked through intellectual and emotional snags, and he provided invaluable comments on each draft. Our feminist partnership continues to sustain me through the ups and downs of the writing process, and so much more.

SERIES EDITORS' INTRODUCTION

Fieldwork, as one of only a few canonical methods of social study, is a messy business placing the researcher deep within the everyday lives of those studied. How sense is made within this buzzing social world is an analytic task highly dependent on the intellectual resources, moral groundings, and cultivated curiosities the researcher carries to (and from) the scene. What is sought, seen, heard, remembered, recorded, and ultimately reported requires a point of view or a stance as to what is of most importance, concern, and value in the examined setting—both to the researcher and to the researched. Values and moral precepts guide our work as surely as they guide our actions beyond research activities but how they do so— and with what results—remain rather unexamined despite a good deal of conversation as to what values and moral precepts best serve a given research community.

Into this conversation comes Sherryl Kleinman's lucid and concrete exploration of how feminist principles can (and should) inform fieldwork and interview-based studies concerned particularly—but not exclusively— with how and why gender inequality in the workplace, at home, and in social interaction is produced and sustained. *Feminist Fieldwork Analysis,* the 51st volume in the Sage Series on Qualitative Research Methods, outlines five useful principles to guide studies of power, gender, and injustice. The writing is personal but care is taken to generalize from the author's own extensive fieldwork experiences to the work of others. The examples are vivid and persuasive. Underpinning the monograph is an engaging narrative that tells how the author gradually moved from a "qualitative researcher to a feminist fieldworker" by learning that overlooking one's own political perspectives and moral imperatives may well have negative consequences on the quality, logic, and reach of the work produced.

At issue in this monograph is not simply the appropriateness of a feminist perspective for understanding gender inequalities but, of equal importance, how a researcher might systematically note, mark, and reflect on the many ways gender inequality is expressed and experienced. A partly tongue-in-cheek tool introduced (and put to use) is the "twinge-ometer," a measured feeling that something isn't quite right in a given situation and anchored typically (and structurally) by inequality and powerlessness. The sensitizing role personal feelings play in research endeavors is a topic Sherryl Kleinman (and Martha Copp) explored in *Emotions and Fieldwork,* (volume 28 of the Sage Series on Qualitative Research Methods) and is revisited and amplified in this work. The earlier monograph is about extending the alertness and sensitivity of fieldworkers to data they might otherwise miss or ignore. This monograph concerns itself largely with putting together a focused, coherent, and appropriate interpretation of data gathered in the field based on a set of sturdy feminist principles and understandings. In the end, the analytic framework developed and illustrated here can help all of us better understand—and thus expose and perhaps alter—the hidden and not-so-hidden workings and costs of inequality.

John Van Maanen
Peter K. Manning
Marc L. Miller

FEMINIST FIELDWORK ANALYSIS

SHERRYL KLEINMAN
University of North Carolina

1. WHAT'S ON THE AGENDA?

> If one admits . . . that social position greatly influences social perspective and if one cannot frame a question without also thereby expressing a perspective, then all science, knowingly or ignorantly, expresses a perspective.
>
> —Sherry Gorelick,
> *Gender/Body/Knowledge*

My mentors in sociology in the 1970s did not teach me a naive view of social science. Fieldworkers, I was told, are never blank slates; our views of the world are always shaped by our identities, group memberships, and values. Thus, to do good fieldwork, we have to know ourselves, including our expectations for and feelings about the people we're studying. We are the "instruments" of research, I was taught, so we had better know ourselves well.

Along with qualitative methods, I learned the perspective of symbolic interactionism. According to Herbert Blumer (1969; see also Mead, 1934)—the scholar who coined the term "symbolic interactionism"—people are not automatons programmed by social forces. Sociohistorical circumstances and situational exigencies shape us, but we can also act back upon them. And action can include everything from resistance to resignation. Blumer's (1969) critique of the application of science to the understanding of human beings also called for close engagement with people rather than distant observation:

To try to catch the interpretative process by remaining aloof as a so-called "objective" observer and refusing to take the role of the acting unit is to risk the worst kind of subjectivism—the objective observer is likely to fill in the process of interpretation with his [or her] own surmises in place of catching the process as it occurs in the experience of the acting unit which uses it. (p. 86)

As a symbolic interactionist fieldworker, I learned to notice patterns of speech, interaction, identity, meanings, and so on. As I became a feminist fieldworker, I did not leave behind interactionist concerns, but linked them to what I had come to care about: the reproduction of inequality, including sexism, racism, heterosexism, and class inequality (see Schwalbe et al., 2000; Thomas, 1993). And analyzing my feelings, in the field or at the desk, began to reveal what Alison Jaggar (1989) calls "outlaw emotions": "our 'gut-level' awareness that we are in a situation of coercion, cruelty, injustice or danger" (p. 161). For many years I had joked with friends about my "twinge-ometer" (Kleinman, 1998), an alarm that would go off when I sensed that something wasn't quite right in a situation. But I had not thought of my twinge-ometer as anchored to injustice until I read Jaggar's work and began to link feminist feelings to the daily experience of inequality.

My move from qualitative researcher to feminist fieldworker was not an easy one. Calling oneself a feminist implies that one has a moral imperative. One is supposedly no longer a researcher looking for truth, however provisional it is and however honest one is about the self that produced the account. As nonfeminist colleagues told me, doing feminist research means that the researcher "has an agenda." It also implies that other researchers do not.

As Sherry Gorelick put it in the epigraph to this chapter, "all science, knowingly or ignorantly, expresses a perspective." Lots of qualitative interactionists would agree with that statement. Interactionism is rooted philosophically in pragmatism, whose key proponents (Dewey, 1929/1984; James, 2000; Mead, 1938) held that knowledge is perspectival. But fieldwork accounts that begin with the word "feminist" or "critical" presumably are less trustworthy than those that do not, implying that only "regular" field studies come close to reaching the highest (scientific) standards.

Because I did not define my earlier work as anything other than symbolic interactionist fieldwork, I felt that my developing feminist analyses were some kind of betrayal to my mentors. I knew I had an agenda: I wanted to understand inequality in order to get rid of it. What I still failed to grasp was that in my previous work I had simply *overlooked* my (not well worked out) political assumptions.

I did not become a feminist fieldworker by participating in consciousness-raising groups, taking women's studies courses, or finding feminist friends.

I wish I had; this might have brought me sooner to a feminist critique, provided support, and made my transition smoother. I came to feminist analysis through the strange route of writer's block, or what I like to call analysis block. Through the long process of picking up and putting down my field notes, analytic memos, and halfhearted drafts about a wellness center I studied when I moved in 1980 to my first job at the University of North Carolina at Chapel Hill, I learned to develop a feminist analysis.

You will read more about Renewal (Kleinman, 1996) later in this book. A fuller account of how my growing feminist consciousness helped me analyze the data appears in other places (see Kleinman, 2002a; Kleinman, 2003; Kleinman & Copp, 1993). I'll provide a synopsis of the changes I went through in that study to give you a sense of where I started and where I ended up.

Renewal, a holistic health center, was constituted by six private practitioners (four white men, two white women) who were paid by individual clients and then gave a portion of their earnings, determined by the board, to the center. The payment was sometimes referred to as rent. The other (educational) part of Renewal was nonprofit and run by three or four staff members (all women) and several volunteers (almost all women). Low-cost classes and workshops were offered to the public through this part of Renewal. Staff members did the office work for the center—including taking phone messages for the practitioners—kept up the physical plant, and put the membership bulletin together. They also produced the newsletter that announced classes. Practitioners received about 30 dollars an hour (in the early 1980s) for their services as psychotherapists, nutrition therapists, massage practitioners, and stress managers. Given Renewal's financial problems (they were almost always in the red), the staff were often unpaid, and received 4 dollars an hour when they did get paid. Overlap existed between the two parts of the organization; practitioners did some volunteer work, often headed major committees, and sometimes taught workshops. Staff, volunteers, and practitioners were represented on the board.

The two key male practitioners, Ron and Jack, were the only remaining founders of Renewal. They had the most power and received the most respect and affection. Jack was chair of the board of directors. Ron headed the committee that determined which workshops and classes would be taught. The board made most of the decisions, from hiring and firing to approving all committee work; having influence on the board was no small matter.

I write this in hindsight. It was not clear to me from the start who really had power. The split structure of Renewal at first struck me as a result of the ineptness of people who had little experience in putting together an organization, not the product of people producing inequality. It took me a long time to recognize the two-class system at Renewal. Why? Because I wanted Renewal to provide the antidote to my job in a quantitative department at a research university. Only a real alternative organization could do that for me. At the same time, I worried that I was violating Blumer's premise: I knew I was not living up to the ideal of having empathy toward participants. Even when I acknowledged the rather glaring inequalities at Renewal, I found myself feeling angry at the underpaid (and sometimes unpaid) staff women. Why weren't they angrier at the practitioners? As I wrote elsewhere (Kleinman, 2003):

> As a liberal feminist at the time, I wanted to believe that women could be successful if we just tried hard enough. This was something I needed to believe as a twenty-seven-year-old female assistant professor—one of two women, both of us without tenure—in a highly ranked sociology department . . . Although I wasn't crazy about the male practitioners at Renewal and distrusted some of their psychologizing, I was preoccupied with the idea that the women were, by the standards of status, money, and influence, failures. I disidentified from them, probably because I needed to believe that I, unlike these women, could achieve the status of the successful men. (p. 218)

When I interviewed the women, I was able to develop empathy for them. At the time I was also reading books on cultural feminism, including Carol Gilligan's (1982) *In a Different Voice* and Jean Baker Miller's (1976) *Toward a New Psychology of Women.* Through these works, I came to see that the staff women at Renewal held what Gilligan calls an ethic of care. They made sacrifices for Renewal because they believed in the "cause" of holistic healing. As I (Kleinman, 2003) put it, "In a short time they [staff women] moved from weaklings to saints in my eyes" (p. 219).

Yet I did not immediately question the motives or behaviors of the male staff members, including Ron and Jack, who were held in the highest regard by everyone. Instead I developed an equal-but-different story: The women wanted a place to find friendship and work on holistic healing, and Renewal served their purposes (at least for a time); the men wanted a homey space to work in that could fulfill some of their desires for informal interactions. If everyone's needs were being met, why should *I* have a problem with it? Wasn't I inappropriately projecting my vision of what Renewal should look like on them?

But my twinge-ometer kept going off as I reread drafts of this version of the story. I felt more empathetic to both parties (practitioners and staff), but I didn't trust the analysis. Fortunately, the acting director of the Curriculum in Women's Studies talked me into developing a new course in Race, Class, and Gender. To prepare for the course, I read the works of Marilyn Frye, bell hooks, Sandra Bartky, and Alison Jaggar (among others). I had never met them, but I heard their voices in stage whispers when I returned to the manuscript, telling me that a better story could be told, one that took power and inequality into account. As I (Kleinman, 2003) wrote later:

> That the women found it acceptable to receive [little money or] no money at all while the practitioners received their pay regularly from clients did not render it fair. That the men benefited much more from the arrangements at Renewal—materially, symbolically, and emotionally—than the women held true whether participants acknowledged it or not. (p. 220)

Reading these authors freed me to write a story that fit with the feminist I had become. Or perhaps I should say that these authors turned me into a better and more systematic feminist. In my analysis of Renewal I came to ask: How did these women and men, with good intentions, manage not to see the ways they contradicted their own ideals? How did they manage to maintain a belief in themselves as good people—those committed to "alternative" ideals—despite their unfair behaviors and hierarchical organizational structure?

Feminist Fieldwork Analysis is a book I would have liked to have read—indeed, needed to read—as I came to write the story of Renewal (see Kleinman, 1996). I hope it will help researchers who share a feminist sensibility but are unsure what to keep in mind as they go about their fieldwork and especially as they write feminist analyses. As feminist researchers, we should be clear about what we mean by "feminist." Knowing one's perspective as a feminist and learning about what other feminist qualitative researchers have written may help researchers make decisions about what to ask and where to look, as well as how to make sense of what we've seen and heard.

The kind of feminist analysis I am talking about is grounded in the ideas of feminist philosopher Marilyn Frye (1983), who uses the term "oppression" to describe the position of women in U.S. society. She conceptualizes the oppression of women as a "birdcage" with systematically related "wires":

> Consider a birdcage. If you look very closely at just one wire in a birdcage, you cannot see the other wires. If your conception of what is before you is determined by this myopic focus, you could look at that one wire, up and down the length of it, and be unable to see why a bird would not just fly around the wire any time it wanted to go somewhere. Furthermore, even if, one day at a time, you myopically inspected each wire, you still could not see why a bird would have trouble going past the wires to get anywhere. There

is no physical property of any one wire, *nothing* that the closest scrutiny could discover, that will reveal how a bird could be inhibited or harmed by it except in the most accidental way. It is only when you step back, stop looking at the wires one by one, microscopically, and take a macroscopic view of the whole cage, that you can see why the bird does not go anywhere; and then you see it in a moment. It is perfectly *obvious* that the bird is surrounded by a network of systematically related barriers, no one of which would be the least hindrance to its flight, but which, by their relations to each other, are as confining as the solid walls of a dungeon. (p. 4)

Frye offers a metaphor, or what social scientists might call a hypothesis. Sociologists and other social scientists have provided the data that document the existence of the wires: sexist language (Hofstadter, 1985; Kleinman, 2002b; Richardson, 2004); the wage gap (Hartmann, Gault, & Williams, 2005; Murphy & Graff, 2005; Reskin, 1988); men's violence against women (Catalana, 2005; Katz, 2006); women's second shift of housework and childcare in the heterosexual home (Deutsch, 2004; Hochschild, 1989b; Tichenor, 2005); women's "third shift" (as I call it) of caring for others (Rubin, 1983; Sattel, 1976); the sexual double standard (Tolman, 2002); women taking their husband's family name; the continual struggle for access to reproductive rights, particularly for poor women and women of color (Davis 1981; Silliman, Fried, Ross, & Gutierrez, 2004); and the list goes on (see Rhode, 1997). Some of these wires are harder to see than others. They are part of what J. Harvey (1999) calls "civilized oppression" (p. 1), whereby physical violence and the enforcement of law are absent.

The flip side of systematic inequality for one group is systematic advantage—or privilege—for the other. As Allan Johnson (2005), a white sociologist, came to recognize in his relationship with an African-American female colleague:

Her misfortune is connected to my fortune. The reality of her having to deal with racism and sexism every day is connected to the reality that I *don't*. I didn't have to do anything wrong for this to be true and neither did she. But there it is just the same.

All of that sits in the middle of the table like the proverbial elephant that everyone pretends not to notice. (p. 7)

It's the feminist analyst's job to recognize and analyze the elephant. Cataloging systematic inequalities for the oppressed group and the corresponding privileges for the advantaged group is not enough. A list is not an analysis; it fails to tell us *how* people live out inequalities. This is where the qualitative feminist's work comes in. Feminist researchers can study hidden inequalities and how the powerful act in ways that mask those inequalities. We can study how women and members of other oppressed groups reinforce the wires of the birdcage. As Sylvia Walby (1990) put it, the experiences of women in everyday life can be "contaminated by patriarchal notions" (p. 18); so can our theories. (More, soon, on patriarchy.)

We can also examine how people resist oppression, individually or collectively. The point of understanding systematic inequality is to learn how to undo it, whether in small or big ways. This raises the question: How do women and male allies resist, and what happens when they do?

As a feminist analyst I also recognize that there are "wires" constraining people of color, people with few economic resources, queer people, people with disabilities, and so on. There are, in fact, many birdcages. Men can't be oppressed *as men*, but they can be oppressed because of their race, class, sexual orientation, and so on (Carbado, 1999; Frye, 1983; Johnson, 2005). A working-class man, for example, may find it difficult to attain the benefits associated with being male. If he has trouble getting a decent job,

> . . . he may have a hard time feeling like a "real man" bonded to other men in their superiority to women. The privileged social category "male" still exists, and he belongs to it, but his social-class position gets in the way of his enjoying the unearned advantages that go with it. (Johnson, 2005, p. 50)

Johnson's statement raises empirical questions for feminist researchers: What happens when members of an advantaged category are denied some of those advantages? Do they try to compensate for their lack of full advantage? Do they question the system as a whole? Having an awareness of multiple systems of oppression is only the start. As Michael Schwalbe (2000) states, "After saying that race, class, and gender are 'systems of oppression,' we are still left to wonder who does what to whom, and how they do it, to keep these systems going" (p. 776).

Analyzing field data within a feminist framework means that we pay attention to inequality. Gender is not a benign set of differing social expectations put on men and on women. Rather, gender is part of a stratification system, and "gender difference can serve as an all-purpose rationalization for gender roles and gender hierarchy" (Rhode, 1997, p. 40). As Judith Lorber (2004; see also Lorber, 2005) put it:

> Gender inequality—the devaluation of "women" and the social domination of "men"— . . . is not the result of sex, procreation, physiology, anatomy, hormones, or genetic predispositions. It is produced and maintained by

identifiable social processes, and built into the general social structure and individual identities . . . The continuing purpose of gender as a modern social category is to construct women as a group to be the subordinates of men as a group. (p. 47)

To rephrase Lorber, we live in a society whose members have inherited patriarchal ideas and practices (Johnson, 2005) and in which men receive a "patriarchal dividend" (Connell, 1995, p. 79). Johnson (2005) argues that patriarchy is societal, "and a society is more than a collection of people. . . . Patriarchy doesn't refer to me or any other man or collection of men, but to a kind of society in which men *and* women participate" (p. 5).

The term "patriarchy" has become unpopular for a variety of reasons (see Bennett, 2006), including a misinterpretation of the word as one describing individual men rather than gendered patterns within a society, and its association with a view of women as victims. But as feminist historian Judith Bennett (1989) wrote:

This division between women as victims and women as agents is a false one: women have always been both victims and agents. To emphasize either one without the other, creates an unbalanced history. Women have not been merely passive victims of patriarchy; they have also colluded in, undermined, and survived patriarchy. But neither have women been free agents; they have always faced ideological, institutional, and practical barriers to equitable association with men (and indeed with other women). (p. 262)

Perhaps some readers hear the word as a reification, as if patriarchy were a Thing that is present or absent. But patriarchy is complex, and, as Johnson (2005) suggests in the title of his book, patriarchy can be "unraveled." Walby (1990) argues that patriarchy can change in *degree* or in *form*. For example, more women now attend institutions of higher education, and this finding could be interpreted as less patriarchy (a change in degree). But new forms of patriarchy might be established to lessen the benefits that women derive from that change. In 2004, the median annual income for women with college degrees was still only about as much as the median annual income for men with high school diplomas (United States Census Bureau, n.d.)— which suggests that a corresponding change in patriarchal form has managed to keep women from translating schooling into better jobs and income.

Barbara Reskin (1988) has shown that as women have gained access to opportunities previously held by men, men have devised new rules to keep women from gaining power. These "new rules" can be seen as a form of institutional backlash against reductions in the degree of patriarchy.

What, then, does patriarchy mean? Johnson (2005) offers a definition: Patriarchal societies—including our own—are male-dominated, male-identified, and male-centered. By "male-dominated," he means that "positions of authority . . . are generally reserved for men" (p. 5). Patriarchal societies are "male-identified" in that "core cultural ideas about what is considered good, desirable, preferable, or normal are associated with how we think about men and masculinity" (pp. 5–6). "Male-centeredness" means that within patriarchal societies "the focus of attention is primarily on men and what they do" (p. 10). These aspects of patriarchy can be studied, including how they differ in degree and form.

As feminist fieldworkers, we can ask: How do these three aspects of patriarchy play out in the settings we study? Are they overt or subtle? Do participants challenge them? What happens when they do? And, to use Ann Russo's (2001) language, are the challenges revolutionary or merely rebellious?

Words like "patriarchy," "oppression," and "privilege" are hard-hitting. They suggest that we live in a society characterized by patterns that hurt particular categories of people and simultaneously benefit others. Years ago, bell hooks (1990) noted that scholars had come to dilute their language when writing and talking about inequality. Her words still ring true:

> *Other* and *difference* are taking the place of commonly known words deemed uncool or simplistic, words like *oppression*, *exploitation* and *domination*. . . .
> There would be no need, however, for any unruly radical black folks to raise critical objections . . . if all this passionate focus on race were not so neatly divorced from a recognition of racism, of the continuing domination of blacks by whites, and (to use some of those out-of-date uncool terms) of the continued suffering and pain in black life. (pp. 51–52)

Unruly radical feminists need to reclaim the words that keep us in sight of patriarchal patterns. Bennett (1989; see also Bennett, 2006, chapter 2) defends the word "patriarchy": "As our [women's historians] language has shifted, so has our thinking . . . As we know from our very first explorations into women's history, what is muted is soon obscured, and what is obscured is eventually forgotten" (p. 254). Strong and precise language helps us remember.

Understanding the adaptability of patriarchy—what Bennett (2006) calls the "patriarchal equilibrium" (p. 4)—and the sometimes hidden nature of sexism and other inequalities, can also help us develop a twinge-ometer for injustice (Kleinman, 1998). Over time, we can thus become better at seeing patterns of oppression and privilege. Sometimes we sense that something is wrong before we figure out what is going on, so it's important to take note of our feelings throughout the research process. In *Emotions and Fieldwork* (Kleinman & Copp, 1993), Martha Copp and I wrote about connections between the researcher's self, her emotions, and qualitative analysis. (I see that earlier work as a companion volume to this book.) In *Feminist Fieldwork Analysis* I focus on the patterns we discover in the field rather than on how we might use our own emotions to analyze those patterns. I hope that this book, along with *Emotions and Fieldwork*, will help feminist fieldworkers develop trustworthy twinges as they do their research.

Feminist theorists and researchers have given us valuable principles that can guide the analysis of social reality. *Feminist Fieldwork Analysis* is organized around five of those principles. The first, "Talk Is Action" (Chapter 2), breaks down the conventional distinction between words and behavior, alerting us to the possible ideological functions and harmful consequences of language. The second, "Similarities Can Be Deceiving" (Chapter 3), highlights common false parallels, whereby people equate the experiences and actions of the oppressed with the experiences and actions of the privileged. The third, "Sexism Can Be Anywhere" (Chapter 4), opens our eyes to the reproduction of gender inequality in same-sex groups. The fourth, "The Personal Is Political" (Chapter 5), reminds us of the importance of linking participants' emotions to power relations. The fifth, "Everything Is More Than One Thing" (Chapter 6), directs us to the intersectionality of race, class, gender, and sexuality.

I culled these principles, mostly in an inductive way, from field studies that examine patriarchal patterns in our society. Looking back, I realize that a discussion of these principles—as applied to fieldwork practice—would have helped me in analyzing Renewal. And they continue to help me as I analyze injustices in my daily life and in the world, a subject I will return to in the final chapter. I have no doubt that there are other principles and hundreds of other studies I could have included in this book. I chose studies that I know best (including my own) to help me show how to put these principles to good use. In each chapter, I will discuss a feminist principle, examine several studies that employ the principle, and provide questions researchers can keep in mind—in the field or at their desks—as they work on their fieldwork projects. My hope is that feminist researchers will find here the sensitizing tools they need to ward off or relieve the kinds of analytic blocks I experienced in my own work.

Doing feminist work, particularly in "disciplines" rather than in interdisciplinary fields like women's studies, still carries a negative connotation. And feminist scholars continue to be labeled within a discipline as the (only) ones who have an agenda. Despite the years of accumulated knowledge about gender and other inequalities in social life (see the notes and bibliography from Rhode, 1997, and Schwalbe et al., 2000, for a start), researchers who study gender (perhaps more so than those who study class, race, and sexual orientation) are supposed to begin a study as if gender inequality has not yet been documented. Deborah Rhode (1997) refers to three patterns of denial of sexism present in our society and reflected in the academy: People deny "the extent of the problems facing women"; people "rationalize women's inequality as a result of women's own choices and capabilities"; and people believe "they personally are neither part of the problem nor part of the solution" (p. 3). I would like to propose that, by ignoring the abundant data on systematic gender inequality as we begin a study, we are committing professional neglect.

For example, I could have stopped my analysis of Renewal by saying that the practitioners and staff gave different meanings to participation in the organization while sharing the goal of being an alternative organization with (some) conventional legitimacy. But doing so would have left out power relations between the two groups. Merely recognizing "power relations," however, did not provide an analysis; the hardest work only began at that point. I still had to show *how* they reproduced inequalities in their behavior, talk, emotional displays, and so on (see Kleinman, 1996). But if I hadn't made gender inequality a part of the story, I would have left out the foundation on which I built the analysis.

In feminist studies, as in other work, "commitment to a set of questions does not imply commitment to a *particular* set of answers" (Gorelick, 1989, p. 351). If we know the answers, why bother doing the study? And because feminists want to understand the world in order to make it better, "we cannot afford to be blinded by our own assumptions" (Gorelick, 1989, p. 351). By recognizing our assumptions and the place of the self in research, feminist researchers "produce less partial and distorted results . . . than those supposedly guided by value-neutrality" (Harding, 1993, p. 49). We are less, rather than more, likely to suffer from "evidence blindness" (Hawkesworth, 2006, pp. 118–141).

Sandra Harding (1987) has made useful distinctions between *methods* ("techniques for gathering evidence" [p. 2]), *methodology* ("a theory and analysis of how research should proceed" [p. 2]), and *epistemology* ("issues about an adequate theory of knowledge or justificatory strategy" [p. 2]). *Feminist Fieldwork Analysis* falls best into the category of methodology. (For lengthier works that connect feminist methods, methodology, and epistemology, see Naples, 2003, and Ramazanoglu, 2002.) I do not discuss nuts-and-bolts techniques for doing a feminist interview or observing interaction (see DeVault, 1999; Sprague, 2005), but instead offer a sensitizing framework that may guide feminist research and the kinds of stories feminist fieldworkers tell. Nor does this book offer a philosophical discussion of feminist epistemology (but see DeVault, 1999; Fonow & Cook, 1991; Harding, 1987, 1993, 2004; Hartsock, 1998; Hawkesworth, 2006; Smith, 1990; Sprague, 2005). Feminist researchers seeking guidance in doing participatory action research (PAR) (Cancian, 1992; Fine, 2006; Sprague, 2005, pp. 182–184), particularly from a feminist perspective, will also have to look elsewhere. However, PAR usually involves an awareness and analysis of inequalities, so the advice offered here may be helpful.

I assume that readers already have learned or are acquiring basic fieldwork skills, such as observing, interviewing, taking notes, and writing analytic memos (see Emerson, Fretz, & Shaw, 1995; Esterberg, 2002; Lofland, Snow, Anderson, & Lofland, 2005). Like other interactionist fieldworkers, I treat data collection and analysis as intertwined rather than as separate activities. The principles and questions found in *Feminist Fieldwork Analysis* can be used at any stage of the research process, including choosing a setting, analyzing an observation, or writing a chapter. Applying what you find in this book might lead you to see things in the field you would not have noticed otherwise, or to see connections between pieces of data that appeared unrelated. Or you might see some of the same things that would have caught your attention anyway, but interpret them in new ways.

All fieldworkers examine patterns of interaction. Feminist fieldworkers still have to figure out which patterns to focus on, how to analyze them, and what to write about them. The studies I chose for this book reflect what I think of as the special contributions of feminism to fieldwork: "Pushing against that which is most taken for granted, feminist inquiry probes absences, silences, omissions, and distortions in order to challenge common sense understandings" (Hawkesworth, 2006, p. 3). By becoming cognizant of patterned absences as much as what lies in our field notes, we can better understand the hidden and not-so-hidden workings of inequality.

2. TALK IS ACTION

It's common in U.S. society to separate words and deeds, and to give a lot more weight to the latter. For example, the expression "Walk the talk" implies that "walking" is the real thing and words are merely talk. But the actions we take (for example, meeting with others to organize an event, writing a petition, or giving a speech) always involve more words. Words are the tools of thought, shaping how we see the world. They point us in particular directions, preventing us from seeing some things and making other things all too clear. With words as our daily tools, we can't help but *do* things with them.

Another expression, "Sticks and stones will break my bones, but names will never hurt me," implies that no matter what we do with language, we can't use it to inflict serious harm. A poster I've seen in a catalog plays off of this cliché to capture the harmful possibilities of language: "Sticks and stones will break my bones, but names will really hurt me." Names—and words, more generally—don't have to hurt, but they can. Racial epithets, slang terms for women, and racist and sexist jokes degrade people of color and women as a group, regardless of anyone's intention. Language can also sustain an environment in which people use sticks, stones, guns, or bombs against others. If we think of a group of people as less than human, it becomes easier to hurt them. The use of "gooks" by U.S. soldiers for the Vietnamese and the use of "hos," "sluts," and "bitches" by men for women in the United States serve as enablers; they don't cause war and rape, but they make it easier for killing and raping to happen.

One does not have to be a *feminist* fieldworker to take words seriously. Words constitute the notes jotted down in the field and the fuller set typed up later. They are the analyses we develop in memos and drafts. Even "head-notes" (Ottenberg, 1990, p. 144)—notes that we should have written down, but didn't—come to us in words. What feminists have taught us is to pay attention to the part that language can play in *reproducing inequalities*, even when the words seem benign or positive (Lakoff, 1975; Spender, 1985). For example, feminists pointed out many years ago that male generics (such as "man," "mankind," and "freshman") make men the norm, render women invisible, and reinforce the idea that it's acceptable to linguistically subsume women under men. But many of the students I teach, including women, claim that "you guys" and "freshmen" are now true generics and thus harmless. I tell them that if "you gals," "you girls," or "you women" were applied to a group of men, the men would feel insulted. "Man" and "men" are still the linguistically superior categories in our society, and "woman" and "women" are derogated (Kleinman, 2002b). And the women in my classes aren't indifferent about "you guys"; they like it so much that they get mad at the possibility of losing it. Being "one of the guys" feels like a raise in status, even if it erases them (as women) at the same time.

If a Martian were to visit U.S. society, no doubt it would notice that women are consistently defined in relation to men (Mrs. or Miss, Mrs. His Last Name) and men are defined in relation to the world (Richardson,

2004). Douglas Hofstadter (1985) takes on the role of Martian-as-anthropologist through his parody of sexist language; he substitutes "white" for "man" to create such terms as "freshwhite," "whitekind," and "you whiteys," revealing the ubiquitous sexism in standard U.S. English that remains invisible to us. Like a good fieldworker, he examines the systematic appearance of male-defined terms and the systematic absence of positive female generics. While not denying racism, he shows how sexism is normalized and made invisible in a way that racism is not.

In this chapter, I will discuss field studies that illustrate the importance of analyzing language for understanding the reproduction of inequality. As we'll see, participants' words (which may include written documents and not only talk) do not stand apart from patriarchal patterns, but are a part of them. In the first half of the chapter, I will look at the legitimating rhetorics of the powerful—how those in the privileged group "explain" their sexist behaviors. In the second half of the chapter, I will look at studies that unravel seemingly benign language practices that reinforce inequality. All of the studies in this section teach us that feminist fieldworkers need to pay close attention to what participants say—or don't say—to fully understand the intricacies of inequality.

The Legitimating Rhetorics of the Dominants

When Terry Arendell (1997) began her study of divorced fathers, she worried that the men she planned to interview would portray themselves in the best light and be unwilling to talk about negative feelings toward their ex-wives because she was a woman and ex-wife. But the opposite occurred. Many of the divorced fathers spoke against their exes; some lashed out at Arendell as if she were a stand-in for their ex-wife. Her study revealed that male entitlement may well follow men into a research project, in how they act toward the researcher and in the stories they tell. Feminists should be aware of both throughout their projects. Here's how they played out in Arendell's experiences with the men and in her analysis.

Sixty-six of the 75 men Arendell interviewed were less concerned about how the divorce affected their relationships with their children than they were about the damage they believed had been done to them, *as men*, by their ex-wives. These men felt wronged, and they justified their hostile feelings for and treatment of their exes and children.

As Arendell (1997) put it, men of different races and classes,

> ... buttressed and buffed their masculine identities through their interactions with me ... they were both presenting themselves as *masculine* persons—defined by them as being competent, assertive, controlling and rational—and working on proving their manhood during their conversations with me. (p. 347)

Her harrowing tale of interviewing these men (Arendell, 1997) shows that they proved their manhood in a variety of ways: Some asked her out; others inappropriately touched her or asked her personal questions. Several men told her how to handle the tape recorder or directed her to questions she should ask. Still others acted aggressively, even violently. As she recounts:

> We [Arendell and a divorced father] were sitting at a diner, with my chair next to and facing away from the back wall. As he recalled how he had picked up his estranged wife by the neck, causing her to struggle, choke, and gag, he thrust his arm across the table and put his hand around my neck. He kept it there as he continued to talk, becoming louder and more excited as he retold the episode. I pushed my chair back as far as it could go but quickly hit up against the wall and so was trapped within his reach. When he finally pulled his hand away, he wagged his index finger directly under my nose as he said, "And I said to her, don't ever make me that mad again. Don't you ever let me get this mad again, don't ever make me this mad" ... Not until the fourth time hearing the tape did I realize that a waitress had approached the table and asked if everything was okay. (pp. 360–361)

The men's reactions to Arendell reflected their understandings about gender—and about their ex-wives. The men held traditional views and voiced these understandings in justifying their behavior. They believed that men and women are different and that the man should head the family. The men said the legal system had worked in their disfavor, even when they had won custody of the children. These divorced fathers categorized their ex-spouse and children as a unit apart from them, even in cases of joint custody. As several men put it, "It's me and them" (Arendell, 1992, p. 162). By setting up the wife-and-children as the enemy unit, the men could justify their hurtful actions. For instance, they said that providing child support meant that they were sending checks to the undeserving woman who just happened to be the mother of their children.

The fathers couched their legitimating rhetoric in terms of *rights*—as men and as fathers. Arendell analyzed the language of "men's rights" as a rhetorical cover for male entitlement. The men expected to control their wives and children, resented that loss of control, and wanted to regain it. As one man told Arendell (1992):

> I am a strong advocate for fathers' rights, for men's rights. I had to fight for my rights as a father; and it cost me over twenty thousand dollars to win the custody fight. But I had to show my ex that I was still in control here, that she couldn't deny me my basic rights just because she got the divorce she wanted. By winning the custody battle, I showed her that I was still in charge. But I knew all along that I would let my son go back to live with his mother once this was over. (p. 166)

One lesson we can draw from Arendell's study is that the word "rights," when used by the privileged, may be a ploy to maintain or take back privilege.

The rhetoric of rights also allowed the men to feel anger—an acceptable masculine emotion—rather than loss or grief. They interpreted their anger as legitimate, even heroic, as they fought against a perceived injustice. Arendell's findings alert feminist researchers to think about how men may use rhetorics rooted in masculinity to go beyond *justifying* sexist behavior, constructing themselves as *honorable*, or even heroic.

Another part of Arendell's analysis of masculinity and fatherhood teaches us that feminist fieldworkers should examine the rhetorics used by those who *reject* sexist legitimating rhetorics and how others in the dominant group react to that rejection. Nine of the 75 divorced fathers in her study responded in more positive ways to the divorce. (Postdivorce custody arrangements did not account for the differences in outlook and behaviors between these men and the traditional fathers.) Androgynous fathers, as Arendell called them, did not think of the family as broken and themselves as separate from the ex-and-children. Rather, they thought of the family as "a network of relationships which, as a result of the divorce, necessitated changes in assumptions and interactions" (Arendell, 1992, p. 170). These men had developed a parenting partnership with their ex-spouse, viewed their children as persons in their own right, and believed they themselves had become better people by increasing their parenting duties (some of the men had parented little before the divorce). These fathers never spoke of men's rights; they didn't consider themselves adversaries of their exes or children. Yet many people, especially other men, pushed these fathers to reframe their androgynous model. As one man said:

Even my father and brother told me to get on with my life, to start acting "like a man" and to let this child go, that my involvement with him would just interfere with my work and future relationships with women. They told me that people were going to think I was a wimp, you know, unmanly, for not standing up to my former wife. (Arendell, 1992, p. 173)

As feminist researchers, we should be aware of whether, and how, other men (and women) try to pull men back into patriarchal patterns. Like the androgynous men in Arendell's study, men who resist patriarchy threaten male privilege *generally*. And this threat is likely to lead to a backlash response on the part of men who go along with (patriarchal) business as usual.

Men who stalk women also see themselves as having lost control over their exes and justify their behaviors rather than show remorse. In these men's view, *she* is the one who has power over *him*. The men cannot see that in reality, *he* controls *her* life. The man's sense of ownership of the woman shows itself in the many references to jealousy in Jennifer Dunn's (2002) study of stalkers. Love and jealousy presumably justify the violence the men perpetrated against their female ex-partners. As one defendant said about the woman he stabbed repeatedly:

> She was my girlfriend and I still love her. I was mad and jealous . . . I went all the way inside her class. And I gave her some candies, and a rose . . . I always gave her presents . . . What she did to me felt bad and that's why, when I saw the hickies, I got mad, 'cause I love her a lot, well, I loved her, I still love her. (p. 42)

This stalker's father echoed that sentiment: "He is just very intense and very serious, and he loved this girl too much" (Dunn, 2002, p. 42). Dunn's study teaches us to be on the lookout for how culturally valued rhetorics—such as romance—may be used by men who engage in intimate violence to legitimate their controlling and harmful behavior toward women. Men's framing of "the problem," as the stalkers' accounts indicate, also positions women as the *cause* of the man's harmful behavior, an idea that permeates the rape culture.

Like Arendell's study of divorced fathers, in-depth interviews with 114 convicted rapists (Scully & Marolla, 1990) indicate that men are willing to speak openly about—and legitimate—the harm they do to women. Using the concept of "accounts" (Scott & Lyman, 1968), the authors found that 47 of the men were *admitters*: They said that they had forced sexual acts on their victims and called it rape. But they also offered *excuses* for their actions, finding ways to deny full responsibility for what they had done. Sixty-seven of the men were *deniers*—they accepted responsibility for the act, but denied that they had done anything wrong. These men offered *justifications* for their actions, finding ways to show that they had acted appropriately in the specific situation.

Admitters claimed that the use of alcohol and other drugs had impeded their judgment; being in an altered state "caused" them to force themselves on a woman. The men also appealed to emotional problems, arguing that anyone who acted this way must be "sick." Like the stalkers, some of these men gave excuses tied to conventional expectations for intimate relationships. For example, one man attributed his crime of abducting and raping a woman he didn't know to his finding out, a few days earlier, that his wife had become involved with her former boyfriend:

> My parents have been married for many years and I had high expectations about marriage. I put my wife on a pedestal. When I walked in on her, I felt like my life had been destroyed, it was such a shock. I was bitter and angry about the fact that I hadn't done anything to my wife for cheating. I didn't want to hurt her [the victim], only to scare and degrade her. (Scully & Marolla, 1990, p. 274)

This man's claim that he had felt "bitter and angry" for not punishing his wife for "cheating" suggests that enacting punishment would have been understandable, perhaps acceptable. That rape is a crime of sexism is shown by his response to his anger at his wife: He found a woman he didn't know as a substitute, as if any woman would do. The authors point out that the popular conception of rape as a psychological disorder rather than a social problem may inform rapists' rhetorics of legitimation. Feminist researchers can analyze psychological, biological, and other kinds of accounts to see how ideas in popular culture, including studies reported in the mass media (especially how they are presented), may be used to justify men's harmful behaviors toward women.

Scully and Marolla's (1990) study shows us how cultural ideas about men and women permeate rapists' talk about their crimes. Deniers tried to justify their behavior by placing the responsibility for their actions on the victim. They positioned the victims as seductresses; appealed to the idea that a woman's "No" really means "Yes"; said that "most women eventually relax and enjoy" the sex (p. 266); claimed that "nice girls don't get raped"; and accepted some of the guilt, but saw what they did as a small mistake (pp. 266–270). As the authors' note, the men's excuses reflect folk ideas (popular notions in the society) about rape, including the idea that if the woman does not fight back or the rapist does not use a weapon, it can't be rape. One rapist who threatened his victim with a bayonet, said:

At the time I didn't think it was rape. I just asked her nicely and she didn't resist. I never considered prison . . . at the time I believed that *as long as I didn't hurt anyone* [italics added] it wasn't wrong. (p. 268)

Treating rape as if it were separate from harm is not uncommon. Newspaper accounts of rape, especially stranger rapes, sometimes conclude with, "There were no injuries." We know what the journalist means—the rapist did not beat up the woman, cut her, or shoot her. But the wording reinforces a view of rape as something less injurious than other forms of physical assault. The feminist researcher can look for patriarchal patterns in such media accounts.

Rhetorics of legitimation aren't always as overt as those that researchers have found among divorced fathers, stalkers, and rapists. But justifications may lie just below the surface, still within reach of the researcher. Asking what the powerful are *leaving out* of their talk may help unpack these rhetorics. The insights that can be gained by paying attention to systematic absences in participants' words can be seen in Carol Cohn's (2000a) interviews with male officers about women's entry into the military. Her study reveals what the men have learned *not* to say, at least at first, in an interview with a female researcher: that they resent women's entry into their previously all-male preserve. Cohn (2000a) analyzed one typical interview in depth, showing how the officer appealed to "objective standards" to legitimate his complaints about women in the military: "They say they want equal rights—well then, they should be held to the same fitness standards we are" (p. 136). This rhetoric hid the officer's strongly negative feelings (revealed later) about having women enter "his" masculine organization.

Appealing to differences between men's and women's physical training (PT) test scores as the reason to keep women out of the military appears fair. Yet Cohn's analysis suggests that feminist fieldworkers might find it useful to develop twinges when the terms "fairness" and "objectivity" are used by the powerful when they talk about their views of women entering male preserves. When the powerful refer to "objective tests" as a "reason" to keep out the less powerful, it is wise to pay attention to the test itself. What does the test measure? Why might some particular test be used rather than something else? Is the test relevant to what the job will entail? Does it predict success later on?

Cohn (2000a) found no clear link between men's fitness standards in the military (the PT test) and specific job requirements. The tests were geared toward (average) male capabilities, and these were not the ones best suited for situations the soldiers would face. Cohn also looked at what is omitted from standard testing. Fitness experts consider flexibility an important part of overall health and fitness, and women, on average, score higher than men on this measure. But flexibility was absent from the PT test, showing that the test itself was skewed toward showing men in the best light and women in the worst. Also, there was variation among men and among women in how they scored on the PT test, but Cohn found no indication that military officers complained when men had low scores. These patterned absences suggest the hypothesis that it was the entry of women into the military—not "objective" scores on tests—that bothered the male officers.

Cohn's (2000a) analysis of the interview with the colonel shows that male officers' appeals to the PT test were a way to keep women out of the military without their having to admit that they believed male military personnel, and men generally, were better than women. For example, as the interview progressed, the colonel said:

> Hold it—they're [women are] coming into the organization, we're all equal, is what we say—and then we're changing the standards. Maybe they needed to be changed, who knows? But still, those were the rules that everybody lived by until that one day when a female walked in that door. (p. 142)

Later, he added, "You joined a male organization, no doubt about it, that's no secret—and everything's gonna change now all of a sudden? It rubs people the wrong way" (p. 143).

Colonel Holmes, when asked directly if women should be in the military, said that 10 years ago, he would have said no. But he now sees that some women are just as smart as the men, and so on. Cohn (2000a) asked him what reasons he would have given 10 years ago. He replied, "Just 'cause this is my male organization and what the heck are they doing, coming in?" (p. 144).

Men in the military are faced with a dilemma: They have worked with competent women and know it is no longer acceptable to say it's unnatural for women to be in the military. Yet they remain angry about losing this male-defined sphere. Referring to tests that are supposedly objective and fair for everyone (that is, both women and men) allows them to believe they are not being sexist, but merely reporting that women just don't do as well and thus should be kept out.

The colonel's account suggests that women won't do as well as men in the military and that such incompetence can have dire consequences. But feminists turn that account on its head. They argue that the problem men have with women in the military—or any other male-defined arena—is not that women will fail to do their jobs as well as men, but that women will do their jobs competently (Johnson, 2005). Perhaps women will even do their work better than men; they will, after all, have a lot to prove.

Women's competence in a male domain suggests that women and men are not that different. Finding similarities between women and men is especially threatening in any occupation, such as the military, that is culturally equated with masculinity. Once the line between "male" and "female" becomes blurred, it's harder to justify male superiority, which is based on the assumption of difference. If women and men aren't so different, then why should men be paid more, have a greater role in the public sphere, and perform less housework, childcare, and emotion work? The studies I have discussed in this chapter thus far show that men, in justifying their prejudices and harmful behavior toward women, focus on assumed sex differences, illustrating Lorber's (2004) point (mentioned in the first chapter) that such differences are not benign, but can be used by the powerful to reinforce and justify male privilege and power.

In addition to studying how men justify overt harm, researchers can examine how men justify the lack of effort they put into working toward gender equality. Francine Deutsch (2004) found that heterosexual men used the following techniques to justify their failure to take equal responsibility for domestic labor: They ignored what was going on around them (for example, a child asking for something); claimed incompetence; praised their wives' skills in doing housework and childcare; appealed to men's and women's "different standards" of neatness and cleanliness in the home; and denied they did so little work. What is striking is the men's use of accounts that flatter their wives:

> I definitely wasn't as good as Roz. Roz's just good. She's good if they get a splinter. She's just good at all that stuff. She's wonderful [as a mother] . . . I feel real lucky to have her as a partner because it takes a lot of the burden off me. (p. 471)

Saying that the female partner is especially skilled suggests that the man—and by extension, men in general—are incapable of learning how to care for children, and that domestic labor is divided up reasonably by who is talented at what. But Deutsch noted a pattern in these so-called talents: Men just happen to be better at doing tasks that require only occasional attention (see also Hochschild, 1989b), while women just happen to be talented at everything else. And Arlie Hochschild (1989b) and Annette Lareau (2003) found in their studies of families that women were almost always the household managers. Women/mothers in heterosexual couples kept track of which child needed to be taken where, whether they were out of bread or milk, and whose birthdays were coming up, including the husband's relatives'. Even when women designated some of the work to their male partners, they continued to do the worry work, figuring out what needed to be done and when.

Some of the men that Deutsch (2004) interviewed shared equally in domestic labor—for a while. What rhetorics did they use to make it easier for them to reduce their labor later on? One man split parenting with his partner in the first few years after the birth of their child, but then, as his wife put it, he "reneged" on their agreement. The husband/father in this couple described his time of equal parenting this way: "It was just great. It completely felt like my own choice and not something that I should do or that I had to do" (p. 474). The language of personal choice, a popular rhetoric in U.S. middle-class society (Schwalbe, 2005, chapter 4), allowed this father to make *other* choices when he felt like it. It's hard to imagine mothers offering the same rhetoric or, if they did, having it taken seriously by their partners or other family members.

Deutsch's study raises important questions for feminist analysts to ask: Who is expected to do what, given their sex, and what are the consequences if someone does not live up to those expectations? The mother who abandons her duties (indeed, the mother whose child merely has unmatched socks) will be held responsible for "bad parenting" in a way that men are not. Who uses the language of personal choice and when? Whose account is legitimated by others and whose is not?

Equal partnerships are possible, but Deutsch (2004) found that this occurs only if the wife/mother insists on it. As one man said about his wife, "Sally is very strong. There's no question about that. I think [the reason for our equal sharing is] partly that Sally makes it that we both share. She feels very strongly about that" (p. 473). Other women too fight for equality in the home, but often meet with a lack of success. Men, Michael Messner (1993) argues, are more likely to give up some of the *costs* of masculinity (for instance, having to be consistently tough and strong) than they are to give up some of their male *privileges* (getting out of cleaning the toilet). We need more research on how men come to value a sense of fairness and take on, and maintain, a commitment to equality.

Ideological Uses of Positive and Benign Language

Feminist fieldworkers might well be primed to look for what lies underneath the accounts of stalkers, rapists, colonels, divorced fathers who rarely see their children, and men who do little housework. But feminist fieldwork studies teach us that we also need to be sensitive to the ideological content and function of language when participants are in groups or organizations committed to nontraditional goals or relationships. The language used by participants may justify differences in privilege and power even when that language seems positive (or neutral) and the fieldworker wants to believe in the group.

For example, in my study of Renewal (Kleinman, 1996), the holistic health center I described earlier, I discovered that everyone, regardless of their position—paid or unpaid, higher paid or lower paid—spoke in ways that emphasized solidarity and the language of equality: "We all care about each other. We're trying to do something different, and that's difficult." How could I dare write an analysis that would criticize such well-meaning statements? Participants did care about each other—they showed it through the affection they displayed before the start of meetings and the tears that fell as they "processed" interpersonal conflicts at retreats. They were making sincere efforts to sustain an organization that differed in some ways from conventional organizations. At the same time, the structure of Renewal was hardly in line with their ideals, and largely reflected members' dual concerns with being both alternative *and* conventional.

As I noted in Chapter 1, there was a status hierarchy between the practitioners (most of them male) and the female staff and volunteers. I came to see that the language of solidarity masked inequalities in the organization. But how did I get there? I learned that it was important to see *who* was making such positive statements as, "We're in this together," and *when*. The key male practitioners made solidarity statements more often than the female staff and volunteers, and they tended to make them after any surfacing of rumblings from staff members to the effect that things were not quite fair in the organization. No one at Renewal was getting rich, and the practitioners did a lot of work on the board. So at first I thought of the language of solidarity as a way for members to deal with chronic budgetary problems; it allowed them to believe they were doing something special and in communion with others. I had trouble stepping back and seeing that the content of their solidarity talk did not benefit everyone equally.

What helped (in addition to reading the feminist work I listed in Chapter 1) was to think about the content of members' idea of fairness or equality. Participants didn't spend time talking about equality per se, so I had to search in their talk for their assumptions. Only when I did this examination could I see that their ideas—shared by both the practitioners and staff— helped maintain the privileged position of the practitioners. This entailed analyzing participants' positive-sounding language, including their talk of caring for each other and sharing alternative ideals.

Members' notions of equality were individualistic and apolitical, almost antipolitical. For them, the "variables" that are the sociologist's stock in trade (sex, race, class, job) were unimportant—these constituted superficial roles that got in the way of authentic interactions and relationships. Members believed it was important to search for the "real self" behind the "mask" of a person's role (see Turner, 1976). Presumably each individual is unique and should be respected equally. But members did not give each other equal respect: Jack and Ron (the two founding members of Renewal) received the most respect and affection and were forgiven quickly for any mistakes they made. In addition, the psychologistic language that members valued—a way of speaking that privileged the male psychotherapists—meant that power relations could be depoliticized and reduced to personality traits.

What did I learn? The language of solidarity (for example, "We're all in this together") might *mask*, *deflect from*, or *compensate for* inequalities. Fieldworkers can ask if members of the oppressed group accept the language of the dominants, or see through it and go along with it anyway, making solidarity more important than their own subordination. We can also see whether subordinates change their view after a while, and examine the conditions that bring about the change.

Language, then, should be linked to relationships, and changes in those relationships over time. For example, the key female staff members at Renewal had intimate relationships with Ron and Jack. Only at the termination of those relationships—initiated by the men—did the women begin to define the men's language as manipulative. At that point, solidarity talk no longer compensated for the women's lack of pay and respect. As Carla, a key member of the staff, said in an interview after she left the organization:

> Ron and Jack would never come right out and say, "We are members of the old society. We are the patriarchs. We are doing something that in this culture gets a lot of money. And we're not gonna be different just because we're in an alternative organization." That's what it *was*, really, but they would never come right out and say that. (Kleinman, 1996, p. 119)

Yet, despite Carla's new language of inequality—patriarchs and money—she forgave the men, largely because she thought Ron and Jack were better than other men:

> I still think that Ron and Jack are such wonderful people in many ways. Yet they had such blind spots. Real blind spots. You've got to understand that they are probably better than a lot of men. They're a lot more human than men on the outside. (Kleinman, 1996, p. 119)

Perhaps Carla wanted to save face; after all, she had been involved with Jack for quite a while. Yet her response also gave the men extra points for being "human." In contrast, Carla and the other staff women at Renewal expected all the women there to be "human." They assumed that care and compassion are female characteristics and thus deserve little praise in the case of women. In fact, they criticized each other and the female practitioners when they failed to live up to perfectionistic standards of humane words and deeds (see Kleinman, 1996, pp. 120–122).

Carla's interpretation of the male practitioners' behavior, even after her "awakening," suggests that feminist fieldworkers must investigate participants' feminist-sounding language. Although Carla used the language of "patriarchs," she nevertheless saw the men as humane, at least when compared to other men. She may have been right. But the lesson is to pay attention to language that fits with feminism as much as to language that is obviously nonfeminist or antifeminist.

Like solidarity talk, neutralizing language can also serve ideological functions. For example, Jackson Katz and Sut Jhally's (1999) content analysis of the media portrayal of the "school shootings" in Columbine showed that journalists used the generic language of "youth killing youth." Katz and Jhally noted that this gender-neutral language hid the facts: In Columbine, as in all previous school shootings, the perpetrators were boys. And until Columbine, all the victims had been girls (see Katz, 2006).

Significantly, male-defined generics ("freshman" and "chairman," for instance) that make women invisible appear in the mass media with regularity. But when exclusively boys or men commit violent actions, suddenly *true* generics—such as "youth" and "kids"—are used. In addition, girls' actions in gangs are framed in relation to their sex ("What Has Happened to Girls?") rather than analyzed in relation to their age. Katz and Jhally argue that the use of true generics in the reporting of the Columbine shootings and similar murders protects boys, men, masculinity, and male privilege.

Such protective language is used especially when the perpetrators are *white* men. Katz (2006) compared the coverage of the rampage at Woodstock '99 with that of the Puerto Rican Day rampage in Central Park in 2000:

> At Woodstock most of the rapists and assaulters were white, and as a result, race hardly ever came up as an issue in the discussion ex post facto. But in Central Park most of the men were African-American and Latino. This no doubt caused some politicians and members of the media to denounce them as "lowlifes" and "thugs"—terms not heard about the alleged (white) perpetrators at Woodstock. (p. 103)

Yet in all the cases that Katz (2006, pp. 91–112) examined, mention of the masculinity of the perpetrators was absent. The language of "youth" and "crowd behavior" hid not only the sex of the perpetrators but also the culture of masculinity that may have prompted the crimes themselves. It is up to feminist analysts to ferret out what is hidden in seemingly neutral accounts, whether in the mass media or in a field site.

Use of the passive voice can serve the same functions as neutral language. People, including journalists, use the passive voice in discussing men's violence against women. Similar to "youth killing youth," the language of "X percent of women were raped last year" hides the fact that all the perpetrators were men. Even the phrasing I used above, "men's violence against women," rarely appears in publications or in conversations. Instead, we more often hear "violence against women." Naming the victims (women) rather than the bulk of perpetrators (men) not only leaves men off the hook; it also reinforces the idea that rape and sexual assault are "women's issues," not men's responsibility. Within the usual framing, the solution becomes a matter of providing more emergency call boxes on campus and more shelters for women rather than preventing men (through education and other means) from harming women. As Katz (2006) wrote:

> People frequently ask why battered women stay with the men who beat them
> . . . It is instructive that few think to ask similar questions about batterers.
> Why do they beat women? Why do so many American men seek to control
> through force the women they claim to love? How might the use of active
> language point us toward answers to these questions? (pp. 111–112)

Without naming the problem as one that is primarily about men and masculinity, feminist solutions can't be sought (or won).

The ideological work of neutral language is also shown in Cohn's (2000b) fieldwork in a community of North American nuclear defense intellectuals and security affairs analysts. The so-called objective discourse there masked the realities of war and turned war into a game of masculine posturing. The language of war in that setting was often abstract, hiding the bloodied bodies of real people. At the same time, the "unacknowledged interweaving of gender discourse in security discourse allows men to not acknowledge that their pristine rational thought is in fact riddled with emotional response" (p. 374). The defense intellectuals interpreted feelings that are culturally defined as feminine (such as sadness) as "emotional." Participants considered such an emotion inappropriate for what they called "the analytic process." Emotional responses that are culturally defined as masculine, such as taking pleasure in aggression and competition (especially winning), were rarely labeled emotional. Thus, these feelings could become legitimated as part of the participants' "analyses" and accepted as indicators of their being realistic about the situation rather than dismissed as emotional.

The language of science can also protect men. Karen Booth's (2004) analysis of scientists' discourse surrounding the source and spread of AIDS in Kenya also demonstrates the ideological functions of "objective" language. She found that published articles highlighted women (prostitutes, in particular) as "high frequency transmitters" of HIV while keeping the men who had sex with prostitutes invisible. This biomedical model, applied by researchers to HIV and published in prestigious medical journals, positioned prostitutes as the transmitters of the disease, men as the bridge between prostitutes and the men's wives, and wives/mothers as transmitters of HIV to their babies.

Yet it was men who visited prostitutes, men who refused to wear condoms (especially with their wives), men who had permission to beat their wives if their wives suggested they wear a condom, and men who said that they "must" have multiple partners. As Booth (2004) commented about the language used by researchers:

> Like criminals, they [prostitutes] are "implicated" in the infections of men. Men are never described as "implicated" in the infection of anyone, including their wives or infants. Only the prostitutes are described as "harboring" various sexually transmitted viruses and bacteria; they are, it is implied, providing safe sanctuary for these evil pathogens, which are just waiting to be transmitted to "susceptible" men. (p. 101)

Booth found in her fieldwork in two clinics in Nairobi as well as in published medical texts that everyone—women, men, policy makers, researchers, and nurses—reinforced this view.

It is especially ironic that researchers posited men as the "bridges" between prostitutes and wives rather than as agents. HIV is much more likely, for physiological reasons, to spread from an infected man to a woman than from an infected woman to a man. The ideology embedded in scientists' language not only absolved men of any blame, but kept all those involved in fighting AIDS from working on changing the behavior of men (condom use, as one particular example, and sexism, more generally). By failing to bring men into the picture in an active way, researchers, policy workers, nurses, and others made it unlikely that strategies for disease prevention and treatment would be successful (Booth, 2004). We learn from this study to look for whether and how "objective" language portrays the role of the powerful as benign, or even casts them as victims, while putting blame on the less powerful.

Talk of differences between men and women as benign (whether appealing to nurture or to nature) may also unwittingly reinforce sexism. Schwalbe (1996) found in his study of the mythopoetic men's movement that these largely straight, white, middle-class men were drawn to Jungian psychology because it helped them deal with their not living up to traditional masculinity. As a result, "The men felt some of the devaluation that women typically experience in our society. Jungian psychology offered relief from the mild victimization they had experienced as gentle men" (p. 57).

The mythopoetic men engaged in rituals that had them crying in front of other men and revealing fears. Although these kinds of talk, emotion work, and rituals are culturally associated with women and femininity in U.S. society, the men dissociated their practices from women and made it clear that this was *men's* work (a term they used, along with "getting in touch with one's deep masculinity" [Schwalbe, 1996]). Thus, their terminology reinforced a division between women and men and failed to give credit to the women who had been doing this kind of psychological and emotional work for years in the women's movement. The female partners of some of the men involved in the group had tried to do this kind of intimate work with them in the past, but the men saw their wives' work as somehow different from "men's work."

The men in this movement knew that men on the outside might define such rituals and interactions as womanly or as something only "sissies" would do. Consequently, they went to great lengths to legitimate their involvement in mythopoetic activities as masculine. They could have characterized revealing vulnerabilities as "human work," thus putting gender itself into question—but they didn't. Rather, they reinstated their identity as men, an identity they did not want to relinquish because it is culturally valued above the identity of women. Thus, even in a setting in which men were trying to challenge the usual norms of masculinity and engage in activities typically associated with women, they framed and spoke about their work in ways that maintained the higher status of men and masculinity. Without recognizing it, they reinforced the gender hierarchy.

As feminist fieldworkers, we can keep an eye out for gender-inflected discourse and see who it benefits and who it disadvantages. For example, the depoliticized language of Jungian psychology kept the mythopoetic men from seeing their systematic benefits:

By promising the men that truth and power could be found within, [Jungian psychology] preempted the careful study of alienating political and economic (and yes, male-dominated) institutions. It also allowed the men to avoid questioning the ways in which their own material ease depended on the very forms of social life that caused their psychic distress. (Schwalbe, 1996, p. 56)

Gendered ways of speaking can vary situationally, and these too can be scrutinized for consequences. For example, various authors have studied women's complaints about the "inexpressiveness" of their male partners, especially when it comes to talking about sadness, fear, or the relationship. As one woman told Lillian Rubin (1983) in an interview:

> I pull for it, I pull hard, and sometimes I can get something from him. But it'll be late at night in the dark—you know, when we're in bed and I can't look at him while he's talking and he doesn't have to look at me. Otherwise, he's just defensive and puts on what I call his bear act, where he makes his warning, go-away faces, and he can't be reached or penetrated at all. (p. 70)

Yet Jack Sattel (1976) argued that men are capable of speaking in intimate ways when it benefits them. Men often speak with emotional sensitivity at the start of a relationship, something they use to seduce women. Once they are in a committed relationship, they often reassert control by masking vulnerability. Sattel acknowledged differences in gender socialization that might account for this behavior, but concluded that men's "inexpressiveness" has more to do with men's unwillingness to be vulnerable than a learned inability. His analysis goes beyond male-female partnerships:

> To effectively wield power, one must be able to convince others of the rightness of the decisions one makes and to guard against one's own emotional involvement and the consequences of that decision. One must also be able to close one's eyes to the potential pain one's decisions have for others and for oneself . . . A little boy must become inexpressive not simply because our culture expects boys to be inexpressive but because our culture expects little boys to grow up to become decision makers and wielders of power. (p. 471)

Sattel then went on to show that working-class men and men of color are more likely to be expressive than middle-class white men. These class and race differences suggest that the language and behaviors of "inexpressiveness" have more to do with preparing particular men for power and privilege in the public sphere than they have to do with male ineptness. Male inexpressiveness becomes a kind of "emotional capital" (Cahill, 1999; see also Jackall, 1988) that can be used to demonstrate that one is the "right man" for the (high-status) job.

***

Feminist analysts should attend not only to terms that are obviously ideological, such as sexist, racist, classist, and heterosexist talk. We can also be attuned to participants' terms or phrasings that appear benign or neutral— including talk about "sex differences"—to see how they fit overall into inequalities that might be present in the group or organization. The case of Renewal (Kleinman, 1996) shows that the language of similarity and solidarity can mask inequalities, depending on the context. Booth's (2004) study shows that abstract language that makes strong distinctions between men and women (and between different "kinds" of women) also has the potential to reproduce inequality. In Schwalbe's (1996) study, we see that a group's use of language that emphasizes men's differences from women— even as members claim that women and men merely have different issues— can also reinforce men's privileges. As in the case of male generics and the language of "objectivity," many sexist terms (and ideas) are unconscious or may even come across as flattering or positive. It's our job not only to notice what dominants and subordinates say, but to see how what they say reinforces or challenges inequality. Becoming aware of the overt and hidden ideological content and consequences of language may also help us analyze how the less powerful *fail* to see inequalities. As in the case of Renewal, participants' apolitical understanding of equality may make it difficult for dominants and subordinates to see inequalities in their midst.

Questions to Ask in the Field or at the Desk

- How does men's sexist talk produce solidarity among men and the exclusion of women?
- In cases where men are called to account, what rhetorics do they use to justify their actions, if they offer justifications?
- Do men dismiss their own behavior as "just joking," argue that "If women can't take it, they don't belong here" (such as in blue-collar work), or appeal to innate differences ("Women aren't meant for this work")?
- Do men make some exceptions, allowing a few women to become "one of the guys"?
- What happens when a woman who fits in calls the men on their sexism? What kind of talk ensues then?
- What language does the powerful group use to justify harming the less powerful group? Do they draw on culturally acceptable rhetorics (for example, romance and victim blaming)?
- Do groups in the setting share a language, or is the language of the powerful different from the language of the less powerful?

- If they share a language, does that sharing become a way to mask, deflect from, or compensate for inequalities? How?
- How does participants' (or subgroups') language downplay inequality or make it hard to see?
- Do participants use the language of objectivity, science, neutrality, or the passive voice? If so, what does this language accomplish for them? Does it hide the power of the privileged group? Does it make the powerful seem benevolent?
- Do the less powerful challenge the language of the powerful? If so, what happens?
- Are there members of the powerful group who develop a language and behaviors that put patriarchal patterns into question? What happens when they do? How do members of the powerful group and the less powerful group react to those challenges?

***

The studies I discussed in the second half of this chapter suggest that women and men can talk in ways that not only reproduce inequality, but also make it difficult for participants, as well as the feminist fieldworker, to notice what's going on. In the next chapter, I look further at the disguises of inequality, examining what sociologists call false parallels.

3. SIMILARITIES CAN BE DECEIVING

Analyses of the neutral- and positive-sounding expressions discussed in the previous chapter reveal that inequality can hide behind a veneer of the benign or the good. Popular media mask inequality by giving us the "good news": statistics on the increased number of women receiving degrees in law and medicine and articles on fathers who do their share of parenting (but see Rhode, 1997). We are left with the impression that things are much better now for women and that equality is around the corner (or has been reached). This makes feminism a hard sell (see Kleinman, Copp, & Sandstrom, 2006).

If someone points out that perhaps there is bad news lurking behind the good news, suggesting that women may not be treated as well as men in law and medicine, someone else might counter by saying that men are probably discriminated against in nursing and elementary school teaching. Such comments can be understood as *false parallels*: statements that draw erroneous analogies between the experiences (and resources, privileges, and power) of the oppressed group and the advantaged group (Johnson, 2005, pp. 167–171; Schwalbe, 2005, pp. 212–217). False parallels are a major way that people—even those with good intentions—reinforce inequality. Whether people are saying that men and women have it equally good or that men and women are both oppressed, they render the history of oppression invisible and erase current inequalities.

In the first part of this chapter, I'll focus on studies that expose false parallels by looking at gender violations—instances where women and men, respectively, step outside the gender box (for example, women in male-dominated fields and men in female-defined jobs). Studies of women and men crossing over gender boundaries provide tests of false parallels (whether the authors intended so or not). If men and women are equally oppressed, then we would expect them to have similar experiences when they enter the preserve of the other sex. Yet the studies examined below indicate that this is not the case: Women in high-status jobs and blue-collar work experience sexism (in overt or hidden ways), and men who enter the "semi-professions" (nursing, elementary school teaching, and so on) find that their male privilege still operates. It *matters* whether the person breaking the usual "barriers" is female or male, because gender itself is a category of inequality. As Johnson (2005) wrote:

> *Sexism* distinguishes simple gender *prejudice*—which can affect men and women both—from the much deeper and broader consequence of expressing and perpetuating privilege and oppression. Without this distinction, we treat all harm as equivalent without taking into account important differences on both the personal and the social levels in what causes it and what it does to people. (p. 170)

By studying gender violations, we are applying an old fieldwork trick: To learn the norms of a group, observe carefully what happens when someone breaks them. In the case of gender violations, we can examine a pattern to see what happens when gender norms are broken, how members of the privileged group and the disadvantaged group react to the broken patterns, and what gender "violators" do in response.

Feminist fieldworkers have also studied false parallels by getting people, particularly those in the privileged group, to talk about their views on gender or race. The second part of this chapter focuses on the false parallels exposed when men talk about gender and whites talk about color blindness. As we will see, making false parallels allows people who see themselves as fair and just to hold beliefs that keep them from engaging in any practices that would work against sexism or racism (and thus threaten their own privileges).

Gender Violations

Wherever fieldwork is done, we might observe gender violations, and we need to examine them carefully. Do such violations challenge the gender order or do they reinscribe it? On the surface it may seem, for example, that the existence of female bodybuilders and male elementary school teachers indicates that patriarchy is disappearing. Today we have more female lawyers, doctors, and professors than we had in the past; this is a break in the old pattern and should be acknowledged. But, as Bennett (2006) found in her study of the history of patriarchy, we need to remain open to the possibility that sexism may persist, perhaps appearing in a new guise (see also Reskin, 1988). Our work has only begun when we notice the existence of men and women who do not follow usual gender scripts.

For example, medicine is the prototypical profession, and it makes sociological sense to think of physicians as being in the more powerful and authoritative position relative to their patients. Yet it's still possible for patients to position the woman as lower because of her sex. Candace West (1992) found in her study of doctor-patient interactions that male doctors interrupted their patients far more often than these patients interrupted their doctors. Yet when the physicians were female, she found the reverse: Patients interrupted their doctors "as much [as] or more than these doctors interrupted them" (pp. 301–302).

That being male is a critical signifier for professional authority is shown dramatically in Susan Phillips and Margaret Schneider's (1993) study of physicians. They found that more than three quarters of 417 female family practitioners reported that they had experienced sexual harassment by male patients. This shows that women can be treated primarily as *women*— whether as sex objects or as people of less general value than men—rather than as *doctors*. Perhaps the harassing male patients were affronted by a woman's claim to professional authority. Their message is something like, "You may have an MD, but you're still just a woman. Don't forget that."

Professional women who move up in corporations are expected, like their male counterparts, to display assertiveness. And this indeed has helped women move up, thus breaking the old pattern in which bosses expected women to be docile. But, as women get closer to the top, the very interactional style that helped them reach that point can be held against them. If bosses and co-workers consider these women too aggressive, the powers-that-be can send them to a program called Bully Broads (Banerjee, 2001). The point of this program, according to its founder Jean Hollands, is to teach successful corporate women "a new set of rules for getting ahead. . . . they must become ladies first." As one woman in the program said—in all seriousness—"I was sent here two years ago because of my intolerance for incompetence" (Banerjee, 2001, p. C1).

The founder of the program makes it clear that the same behaviors would be acceptable in *male* executives, thus showing that it is false to assume that women who make it far up the ladder will be treated just like men. She justifies the treatment women receive: "We don't [get the same consideration men do]. So what? We've only been in the work force as leaders for 50 years. Men have a 600-year head start on us" (Banerjee, 2001, p. C1). By participating in the program, these corporate women learn to cry, play dumb, and use hesitations in speech when interacting in the workplace, especially with men. As one participant said, "Some of the, um, modifications Jean [Hollands] suggested have helped me. . . . I just said 'um.' I never used to say 'um.' But I'll pause more now" (p. C1).

Sexism in the case of Bully Broads is blatant, but it's important to think about what alternative response there might be to situations in which men at work feel uncomfortable with women's assertiveness. For instance, is it unthinkable that the distraught men would be sent to a program for "Sexist Men" who cannot deal with women as equals? Engaging in this thought experiment—substituting men for women—can help researchers see the extent of sexism. As in other realms, it is women who are expected to adapt if men act in sexist ways.

We can see how sexism is normalized by engaging in another thought experiment: substituting race for sex. In a letter to the editor, Lydia Tolar (2001) wrote,

> Can you imagine if, like Bully Broads' founder Jean Hollands, we rationalized such an obviously discriminatory program by excusing the discomfort of insecure whites with confident, successful African-Americans through comments like, "Can you get over a 400-year history of being socially dominant? This is a deeply embedded thing in whites." (p. A10)

Tolar added that if "Bully Blacks" existed (and note that "Blacks" is not the equivalent pejorative of "Broads"), black employees would no doubt file a lawsuit. Such thought experiments help feminist fieldworkers analyze the ingrained assumptions of men and women in the reproduction of patriarchal patterns.

That male advantage and female disadvantage persist even when women make their way up the occupational ladder underscores Reskin's (1988) point (mentioned in the first chapter): When members of oppressed groups start to do better and enter privileged spheres, the privileged group will change the rules to make it more difficult for them to succeed. As field-workers, we should be on the lookout for overt and hidden new rules. These expose the lie of the false parallel: Women may enter a high-status male-defined domain, but their experiences are not the same as those of men.

Women who enter blue-collar jobs and other male preserves also face "old" sexist patterns, including a variety of forms of discrimination and sexual harassment. In two studies of women working in coal mines (Padavic, 1991; Tallichet, 1995), the authors found that the men used the ideas of femininity and hypersexuality to discredit women. For example, some men acted as if the women were too physically weak to do the work and occasionally offered help when the women didn't need it, sending the message to supervisors that women are incapable of performing the job. Irene Padavic, who shoveled coal as part of her study, found a pattern of paternalism:

> Several instances stemmed from the supervisor's fatherly concern. Once it led him to threaten to transfer two teenage contract employees who were, he felt, spending too much time with me. His concern was not that our productivity was suffering (we all had completed our work for the day and "hanging out" at such times was generally acceptable), but that I could not take care of myself around two teenage boys because, as he warned me, "you know how boys are and what's on their mind" . . . He also pointed out that although some women can do the job as well as a man, he did not expect me to be able to because I was too small. (I am 5'4," of medium build, am in good physical condition, and had lifted weights in preparation for the job.) In one instance, his special concern for my safety led him to tell me that although he was not allowed to administer first aid, he would do so in my case, explaining that although he would feel terrible if any of his people got hurt, he would feel even worse if it were I. He described in detail how dangerous the plant was ("if your long hair gets in a gear . . ."). (p. 286)

Under the guise of caring about Padavic more than he did the male workers, the supervisor made it more difficult for her to act like any (male) worker. At the same time, he and the male workers ignored the woman who was bigger and stronger than Padavic, making fun of her behind her back. Her violations of femininity in size and demeanor were a problem for the men because she challenged their masculinity, and, by extension, one of the beliefs—(all) men are stronger than (all) women—that undergird male privilege.

Suzanne Tallichet (1995) found the same behavior in another coal mine and, importantly, linked these behaviors to the reproduction of job inequality.

By isolating the women, male supervisors denied them opportunities to develop the working knowledge, typically offered by co-workers, that is crucial for doing the job well. This lack of knowledge was then used against the women when they sought promotions. In addition, Tallichet (1995) found that the men reinforced gender inequality by giving women the work of assistants or helpers, akin to demoting them:

> Sunday I carried cinder block and rock dust behind them. I cleaned up the garbage, I carried their junk to them if they wanted it. It's just like you're a gofer or something. When they set up, they throw down everything. It's up to us to go clean up their mess. I know all the women experience the work discrimination because most of us are gofers, hard manual labor. (p. 708)

Some of the work assigned to the women by men was sex typed, akin to housework:

> I've had bosses that treat you worse than the men. They make you go pick up things. When I was general inside labor, it didn't matter what section I went to; they'd expect me to clean the dinner hole. (Tallichet, 1995, p. 708)

Fieldworkers should be alert for the double bind in their studies of women entering male domains (Frye, 1983). As Tallichet (1995) found, women who cursed as much as men in their blue-collar jobs risked losing the respect of their male co-workers and supervisors. But if they didn't curse or called the men on their swearing, the women put themselves in the "feminine" category, synonymous—to the men—with not being real (that is, tough) workers.

We can also be sensitive to the way that men's behavior marks women in "their" domain as sexual objects first and workers second. For example, men often made passes at women in the mines and spread false rumors of having had sex with them. Sometimes the men labeled female co-workers lesbians (in a pejorative way), especially if the women had turned them down for sex. In either case, the men made comments about the women's sexuality to *undermine* them in their role as workers.

Yet this did not mean that men refrained from sexual talk about themselves. To examine whether a false parallel exists, one examines whether the same behavior occurs in both men and women, and the responses to it. In the mines, men's talk among themselves regarding their alleged sexual exploits reinforced or *enhanced* their status.

To put a false parallel to the test, researchers can ask, as Christine Williams (1995) did: What happens to men who go into female-identified occupations? Do men have to prove themselves as much as women going into male-dominated occupations? In her study of nursing, library science, elementary school teaching, and social work, Williams found that men's position as a numerical minority *upped* their status. The men largely received positive treatment and experienced what she calls a ride on the "glass escalator." The men's advantages began in graduate school, where, except in the study of nursing, many of the professors and administrators are men. In fact, male faculty members often made a point of initiating contact with male students and "explicitly encouraged [them] *because they were men*" (p. 69). As one male student told Williams after she asked about encouragement the men received in graduate school:

> Yeah. Both of these guys, for sure, including the Dean who was male also. And it's an interesting point that you bring up because it was, often times, kind of in a sign, you know. It wasn't in the classroom, and it wasn't in front of the group, or if we were in the student lounge or something like that. It was . . . if it was just myself or maybe another one of the guys, you know, and just talking in the office. It's like . . . you know, kind of an opening-up and saying "You know, you are really lucky that you're in the profession because you'll really go to the top real quick, and you'll be able to make real definite improvements and changes. And you'll have a real influence," and all this sort of thing. I mean, really, I can remember several times. (p. 70)

In addition, men in these occupations experienced preferences in hiring. And bosses often bumped them up into administrative posts. This was true even for men who preferred to remain, for instance, elementary school teachers rather than to become administrators. The higher-ups assumed that the men were more competent than the women. As one of Williams's (1995) male teachers put it: "If you're a mediocre male teacher, you're considered a better teacher than if you're a female and a mediocre teacher. I think there's that prejudice there" (p. 105).

The men that Williams interviewed were aware of the special treatment they received. Yet their awareness did not lead them to value the "feminine" aspects of the job or the women they worked with. The men knew that they were in a feminine-typed occupation and found ways to disidentify from the cultural association of femininity with weakness. In addition to having bosses push them into administration (defined as masculine work in our society), some of the men also pushed *themselves* as a way of dealing with the stigma of being in a female-defined profession. A male social worker who worked in administration told Williams (1995):

I think . . . because I'm a man, I felt a need to get into this kind of position. I may have worked harder toward it, may have competed harder for it, than most women would do, even women who think about doing administrative work. (p. 136)

This quotation shows that he assumed that women would be less competitive than men. He and other men sought to distance themselves from women in ways that justified their superior status as men. As Williams (1995) concluded: "Paradoxically, men in nontraditional occupations can and do actually support hegemonic masculinity, and end up posing little threat to the social organization of gender" (p. 141). The men's minority status in the field became a benefit. This contrasts with the costs women experience due to their minority status in male-defined jobs and professions.

Williams studied men who had opportunities to move up in female-defined occupations. What happens when men enter "feminine" occupations that have no career ladder? Is their experience the same as that of women in these low-status jobs? Kevin Henson and Jackie Rogers (2001) asked these questions in their study of male (and female) clerical temporary workers. They found that:

. . . the type of gender one must "do" in clerical temporary work is primarily white, middle-class, heterosexual femininity . . . it is nearly impossible to do this brand of femininity appropriately if you are a man or a woman of color. (p. 221)

The men, almost all of whom were white, had particular difficulties with the job because of the feminine emotional labor expected of them (Hochschild, 1983): acting in a deferential and nurturant way with bosses, co-workers, clients, and those in the employment agency. The men were taken aback by this requirement; as white men, they had little previous experience. One male temporary worker put it this way when describing a female superior:

At my long-term assignment, this one permanent secretary was out sick. I had my own desk and I had things that had to be done. And this woman comes up to me and she hands me a stack of photocopying to do. And I said, "Excuse me." And she said, "Well this is for you to do." And I said, "Well, thank you, but I have my own work to do. This work has to be done by 5." And she goes, "Well, you are just a temp and blah blah blah blah blah." I said, "Wait a minute. I am a temporary worker, but I do have a desk and assigned work that has to be done." And she threw this little fit. And throughout the day she was really terse and really just a real bitch to me . . . She was just awful. You know that whole mentality of "just a temp, just a temp." (Henson & Rogers, 2001, p. 234)

Some of the men were willing to lose their jobs rather than to show deference. Like the men in the semi-professions Williams (1995) studied, they found ways to distance themselves from this "feminine" work. For example, they "renamed and reframed" the job, studiously avoiding the term "secretary." (Others in the workplace often colluded with this strategy.) They also developed cover stories to explain why they didn't have permanent, better-paying jobs, as is expected of white middle-class men—one man said he was a writer, another said he was an actor. Fieldworkers who are studying men in "female" jobs should be sensitive to such disidentifying strategies.

Henson and Rogers (2001) made sure to compare the stories told by the men and the women, a good fieldwork strategy for seeing if there are false parallels at work. They found that some female temporary workers also had cover stories, but these reflected an anxiety about class, not gender. People in the workplace rarely pushed women for explanations for temping, because that kind of job was already marked as female. Overall, the authors found that the men's resistance to identifying with the job reinforced the gender typing of temporary clerical work as feminine. The men's strategies suggested that they were the exceptions to the rule of temping as a job for women.

Another fieldwork lesson from research on male temps is that studying the deviant case of *male* temporary workers may reveal societal expectations for *women*. As Henson and Rogers (2001) wrote, male temporary workers were "curiosities to be pitied, [but] the low-pay, impermanence, and dead-end nature of these jobs [were] seen as natural or unproblematic for women" (p. 227).

The men in the semi-professions and in temp jobs had no interest in changing the "masculine" (white and middle-class) culture of the workplace. What happens when we study a setting in which white women and men are present and the style of interaction valued in the group—and even the members' belief system—appears to favor white femininity? When I studied Renewal (Kleinman, 1996), I noticed that members' values, such as talking about one's feelings of vulnerability, being compassionate and cooperative, and rejecting hierarchy and competition, fit cultural associations with "womanliness." Wouldn't women and men in this setting consider female participants to be those in-the-know? This is a particularly good test of whether male privilege and female disadvantage operate, even when the setting appears to favor women. I found that the *men* received the most accolades when they behaved in "womanly ways" and that members readily excused them for doing anything that might otherwise have been called masculinist.

For example, Ron, one of the key male practitioners, sometimes fell silent rather than talked about his feelings of vulnerability at retreats. (He had no problem expressing or talking about his anger.) Instead of distrusting him for keeping his feelings to himself, participants forgave him, saying he was so "deep" that it made sense that he wasn't ready to deal with his "emotional wounds." In addition, any disclosure on Ron's part led others to thank him or even resulted in spontaneous applause. All of his expressions, including anger, were taken as signs of progress he had made toward his self-development.

As Jane, a key staff member, said in an interview, "Ron is difficult to deal with at times. But I think he's got a real gift, too, and I think a lot of him. I feel he's real trustworthy underneath it all and part of the family" (in Kleinman, 1996, p. 119). On the other hand, when Jane withheld her feelings at a retreat, she was told, "I want you to look at how much power you have in staying silent. What are you waiting for? Don't you know that we love you?" (p. 87). At other times, when female staff members fell silent at retreats, others accused them of pulling a "power play."

The male practitioners could use the privileged psychologistic language against the female staff, translating the women's complaints—once the staff started complaining—into blame. For example, when the staff women said that they had paid basic bills of the center instead of themselves and that something needed to be changed to keep this from happening in the future, Jack told the women, "I think you and Jane don't take care of yourselves as well as you might" (Kleinman, 1996, p. 111). Because he was a founding member of Renewal, a psychotherapist, and someone skilled in the language of the psychology of emotions, his words had authority.

Male privilege followed the men into this setting. That the men had pursued holistic healing rather than more conventional careers won them points with the women. Because they were white middle-class men, others (especially the women) assumed that they could have used their privileges to gain more status and money in other fields. Consequently, the women regarded the men as having made *sacrifices* for the cause of holistic health, thus upping their status in the organization. The staff women, on the other hand, were seen by the men, and by each other, as merely doing "women's work," which had little value. Being women, the female staff had no privileges to sacrifice; hence, they could not gain extra points for giving up any privileges. Another false parallel was revealed by both men's and women's responses to the few women who worked as practitioners at Renewal. They did not receive the same points as the male practitioners but were instead looked upon as selfish careerists.

Renewal, being a holistic health center, was coded as feminine, and was thus regarded in the wider community as less legitimate than a medical establishment, coded as masculine. Both women and men at Renewal valued the two central male practitioners and thought of them as representing Renewal. All members relied on the hidden valuation of men to legitimate the feminine-typed center to the wider community and to themselves. The men also had privileges by being alternative, straight, romantically available white men. The women at Renewal wanted to be involved with men they perceived as sensitive and humane. Such men were a scarce resource. Consequently, the women found themselves in competition over Ron and Jack. This made it difficult for female staff members to see the men's imperfections and easy for them to criticize each other. Thus, the privileging of men and masculinity operated even in a setting in which members had presumably *rejected* the values that uphold a patriarchal culture.

False parallels may also be revealed in the private sphere. Just as it is "natural" for women to be temps or to do the "housekeeping" at work, it is expected that they will have major responsibility for the second shift of housework in the heterosexual household (Hochschild, 1989b), even when both the male and the female partner work outside the home (Brines, 1994). Women are also held responsible for what I call the third shift; they are supposed to take care of relationships with men, children, elderly parents and relatives, and so on. What happens when men do this work? Do women give men extra points for participating in the third shift? How do other men react? Perhaps men consider these male partners "wusses" or "whipped" (as we saw earlier in the case of androgynous fathers), indicating that it is men acting "like women" that undergirds their responses.

And what happens if a woman refrains from being nurturant and expressive? Both women and men might call her "cold," "bitchy," or "an iron maiden." Women can be treated as "Bully Broads" in interpersonal relationships as well as in the workplace. It is the feminist fieldworker's job to look at these "deviant cases" and examine the responses to and consequences of these gender violations.

An interesting twist on stepping out of gender scripts and the exposure of false parallels is shown in Hochschild's (1989a) examination of what she calls the economy of gratitude in married, two-earner households with two young children. In the case of Nina and Peter, Nina, a high-level executive, made three times as much money as Peter, who managed a bookstore. Given our capitalist context, one might expect Peter to do more household labor than Nina. The parallel might be stated this way: A person who makes a lot of money, regardless of sex, has the most power in the relationship and will do the least amount of housework. In Nina and Peter's case, Nina also gave Peter the opportunity to have a job he valued, even though it provided only a small income.

But here's what happened: Nina did the bulk of the housework, and *she* was grateful to *him* for "allowing" her to work at a busy, well-paying job. Given the gender rules in the United States, a man is supposed to do better in the sphere of work than his female partner (Hochschild, 1989a):

> Peter felt proud *for* Nina, and proud *of* Nina, but he could not feel proud *because* of her; he could not *share* her new status. He could not feel "given to" by her . . . Indeed, her rise in status actively reduced his—not in Nina's eyes, but in the eyes of his relatives and neighbors and old friends—and among them, especially the men . . . Peter treated her salary as a miserable secret to manage. They did not tell Peter's parents—his father, Peter explained, "would die." They did not tell Nina's parents because "she even out-earns her father." They did not tell Peter's high school buddies back in his rural home town in Southern California because "I'd never hear the end of it." Her salary was treated as a deviant act, even like a crime. (p. 104)

Nina did most of the housework to make up for outearning her husband, thus protecting his masculinity in (at least) the "feminine" realm of the home. Both Nina and Peter were violating gender norms, but it was Nina who was supposed to protect Peter from others' criticism, particularly that of other men (see also Brines, 1994; Tichenor, 2005). Hochschild's study reveals the persistence of patriarchy and the ability of men and women to collude in keeping things the same, even as they change.

Denying Inequalities

A common false parallel I encounter in teaching about sexism is students' belief that women and men are *equally* hurt by "gender roles." What is missing from this equation is an acknowledgment of history and the systematic advantages that accrue to men—as men—and the corresponding disadvantages that accrue to women—as women (Frye, 1983).

For example, Frye argued that while a man may suffer individually from the dictum that "men shouldn't cry," men *as a group* benefit overall from this rule. Men created this rule, though women may also reinforce it. Why would men have made this rule? Because people who don't cry can presumably be counted on to act rationally and objectively, maintaining composure under pressure. Unlike people who might fall apart at the first sign of trouble, members of the "unemotional" group are the ones deserving of major responsibilities, respect, and greater pay. Men maintain the guise of invulnerability in order to show other men that they are fit for exercising power (Sattel, 1976). Hiding one's vulnerabilities also gives one an edge in competition; others must know where your jugular is in order to go for it.

Making false parallels is not necessarily the domain of conservative angry white men. In his field study of the mythopoetic men's movement, Schwalbe (1996) found that these liberal gentle men believed that women and men are equally oppressed by some "impartial culture, and neither group was responsible for oppressing the other" (p. 146). By reifying "society," the men denied that oppression is about the relationship *between* groups, and that men as a group are privileged at the expense of women. The men spoke as if there were an abstract society out there that rains down equally oppressive gender expectations on women and men.

How did these men justify this false parity? The mythopoetic men engaged in "strategic anti-intellectualism" (Schwalbe, 1996, p. 147). As intelligent, educated men, participants in this movement had the capability—and the resources—to distinguish between the oppression of women and the costs to men of trying to living up to masculine ideals. As Johnson (2005) put it:

> Men do not suffer because maleness is a devalued oppressed status in relation to some higher, more powerful one. Instead, to the extent that men suffer as men—and not because they're also gay or of color—it's because they belong to the dominant gender group in a system of gender oppression, *which both privileges them and exacts a price in return* [italics added]. (p. 24)

Fieldworkers should listen when people call a group on their false parallels. In the case of the mythopoetic men, any allusion to the oppression of women led them to engage in a rhetorical game that implied that men and women are equally oppressed. For example, Schwalbe (1996) culled the following items from typical mythopoetic publications:

> Male infants suffer a 25 percent higher mortality rate than female infants.

> Men must register for the draft or face prison. Women are exempt.

> Men constitute 95 percent of all job fatalities, even though women are 50% of the workforce.

Men are almost 100 percent of those assassinated for political reasons.

Men are 75 percent of the homeless.

Men die, on average, seven years earlier than women.

Men are 95 percent of all prison inmates.

Men are 80 percent of all homicide victims. (pp. 147–148)

The mythopoetic men did not investigate the roots of these facts. About 50% of the 7-year mortality gap between women and men can be attributed to smoking. The rest can be attributed to behaviors that fit hegemonic masculinity: not seeking medical care, heavy drinking, industrial accidents among working-class men, and lack of friends in old age. (For a fuller discussion of the costs of masculinity to men's health, see Sabo, 2004). Schwalbe (1996) argued that the men could have delved into epidemiological sources of this gap, but that it was not in their interest to do so. They wanted to refute feminism rather than "think seriously about the real sources of pain in men's lives" (p. 149).

False parallels can also be found in studies of racism. Melanie Heath (2003) studied the Promise Keepers, a Christian movement that calls on men to reestablish their responsibilities in the family. The Promise Keepers saw themselves as good people for seeking "reconciliation" with men of color, but ignored racism in U.S. society and the privileges that accrue to white people, regardless of their degree of prejudice. As one white man put it in describing a speaker at a Promise Keepers rally: "The message is that reconciliation cuts both ways—black, white, or whatever color you are, it doesn't matter in the eyes of God. That's the message of the Bible" (p. 439). By adopting a color-blind strategy, the white men acted as if the only thing needed to end racism is for white men and men of color to join hands and seek answers within themselves rather than engage in political action. Such statements as "Reconciliation cuts both ways" sounded nice but in fact hid a false parallel. This expression denied the existence of white men's privileges while reinforcing their belief that they were good Christian men for having had contact with men of color.

The implications of false parallels for reproducing inequality, especially as they show themselves in color-blind language, have been analyzed by David Wellman (1993), Eduardo Bonilla-Silva (2003), and Ruth Frankenberg (1993). These researchers analyzed color blindness as a way that white women and men maintain an image of themselves as unprejudiced while maintaining white privilege. All three authors defined racism (in the United States) as a system of white advantage. They interviewed white people and discovered how whites defend their racial privilege in ways that allow them to believe they are not "explicitly contradict[ing] egalitarian ideals" (Wellman, 1993, p. 53). This allows whites to express views that are seemingly nonracist or antiracist while arguing against policies (for example, affirmative action) that would reduce racism—and thus reduce some of their privileges as white people. Like the Promise Keepers, many white people use what Frankenberg (1993) calls a color- and power-evasive strategy (p. 142): They say they do not see color, and this presumably makes them good (unracist) people. Yet, as the three authors argue, such rhetorics ignore not only a history of the oppression of people of color but *continuing* inequalities in education, employment, housing, and so on.

Bonilla-Silva (2003) discussed the strategies white people use to feel good about themselves while arguing against institutional changes that would help people of color. The main strategy he discovered was "abstract liberalism." People use

ideas associated with political liberalism (e.g., "equal opportunity," the idea that force should not be used to achieve social policy) and economic liberalism (e.g., choice, individualism) in an abstract manner to explain racial matters. By framing race-related issues in the language of liberalism, whites can appear "reasonable" and even "moral," while opposing almost all practical approaches to deal with de facto racial inequality. (p. 28)

As Bonilla-Silva, Frankenberg, and Wellman found, many whites who were against affirmative action used the language of abstract liberalism to oppose it. One of Ruth Frankenberg's (1993) interviewees put it this way (a response typical of white people in the three studies):

I resent it particularly because I feel that people should be considered for who they are as a human being and not as this, that, or the other—who you are, regardless of outside trappings—[there's an] inner person, shouting to get out. (p. 149)

Appealing to humanism made it seem as if race, in U.S. society, doesn't really matter, thus implying that whites and people of color are in the same position (a false parallel). Much like the members of Renewal, Frankenberg's (1993) interviewees denied inequality by construing the individual as someone unaffected by racial oppression or privilege. Such appeals made it difficult to recognize that affirmative action programs are meant to make up for years of racism and sexism (Fish, 1994). The lesson here is to remain open to the possibility that people who claim egalitarian ideals and an image of themselves as fair may still reproduce inequalities. They may ignore their privileges and avoid taking action against inequality by appealing to false parallels and self-serving blindness.

***

Popular false parallels may inform what we study—for example, by leading us to examine what happens to men who choose or find themselves in settings coded as feminine and women who choose or find themselves in settings coded as masculine. Will the particular gender violation "denaturalize" the cultural link between sex and gender, or will participants find ways to reinforce gender differences and the male advantages and female disadvantages that go along with them? The mere presence of a woman in a position of authority or at a job associated with "masculine" strength might lead to interactional backlash on the part of men. Yet the presence of a man in "female" workplaces may lead him to receive special points from co-workers and supervisors rather than suspicion.

Fieldworkers should be on the lookout for people's uses of false parallels in every setting. How might we know that we've encountered a false parallel? If a participant points out a wire on the birdcage of the oppression of women (for example, that women in advertising are consistently portrayed as skinny) and someone responds with a comment suggesting that men are suffering equally by that wire (for example, "Men are expected to look a certain way, too"), probably the statement is a false parallel. We may also find *ourselves* falling into false parallels. The questions below should help researchers figure out if a false parallel is operating.

Questions to Ask in the Field or at the Desk

• When someone says that men and women suffer equally from any particular gender expectation (or if we find ourselves making that same point), we can ask: Who created the gender expectation or rule? For example, if we hear the statement that both men and women are pressured to look good, we should examine the content of "looking good" for each sex. Men, for example, are expected to be larger and more muscular and women are supposed to be thin and fit. Who benefits from these expectations? Do these expectations reinforce male dominance and female subordination? If so, we are facing a false parallel and can analyze how it denies gender inequality and unintentionally buttresses the privileges of the powerful group. We might also ask: What are the consequences if men do not live up to the expectation? If women do not live up to the expectation? And finally, what would have to happen for the false parallel to become a true parallel?

- In the case of gender violations, we can ask: What happens to women who have moved into positions usually occupied by men? What patterns do we find there? Do bosses and co-workers give them the same respect they give men? Has discrimination against women in the workplace ended for those women, or does sexism persist, perhaps in a new form?

- And what happens to men who find themselves in female-defined jobs (or other spaces)? Are the bosses men or women? Do bosses treat the men with respect or look on them suspiciously? If male advantage carries over, how does it play out in interactions with men and women?

- In the interpersonal realm, we can ask: What happens when men do their share of the third shift? How does the female partner react? How do her female friends, and the women in the neighborhood, react? Do they give these men extra points? How do other men react? Do men consider him a rate buster, giving other men a bad name?

***

Fieldworkers who study settings in which women and men hold traditional roles will probably be on guard for sexism (for example, male bosses' treatment of female secretaries). We may be more surprised to find overt or covert sexism in the case of gender violations, especially when women engage in activities or join occupations long held by men. These are, after all, supposed to be instances of success. Whether examining gender conformity or gender violations, we can study the patterns of interaction between women and men and how these patterns reproduce or challenge inequality. But is it possible to study inequality when only men are present or only women are present? The next chapter explores feminist studies that reveal the reproduction of gender inequality in same-sex groups.

4. SEXISM CAN BE ANYWHERE

I've often heard faculty and graduate students say, in my predominantly quantitative department, that "you can't study gender unless you have data on women and men." If one treats gender as a variable, then that belief makes sense; comparisons are necessary to see if gender has an "effect." Yet "some of the most extreme displays of 'essential' womanly and manly natures may occur in settings that are usually reserved for members of a single sex category" (West & Fenstermaker, 1995, p. 31). In this chapter I'll examine qualitative studies on the reproduction of inequality in same-sex groups and in settings where only a few members of the other sex are present.

Analyses of all-male groups reveal that men *reproduce* hegemonic masculinity or find ways to *compensate* for its loss. As Michael Kimmel (in Katz, 2006) has argued, "In large part, it's other men who are important to American men; [they] define their masculinity, not as much in relation to women, but in relation to each other. Masculinity is largely a homosocial enactment" (p. 119). And this relationship among men (particularly heterosexual men) is based on a cycle of control and fear (Johnson, 2005):

> Men pay an enormous price for participating in patriarchy. The more in control men try to be, for example, the less secure they feel. They may not know it because they're so busy trying to be in control, but the more they organize their lives around being in control, the more tied they are to the fear of *not* being in control. (p. 55)

Feminist fieldworkers can look for the strategies men use in reinforcing or reclaiming that sense of control and the harmful consequences of those strategies for both women and men.

Women did not create the wires of the sexist birdcage, but they can still *reinforce* them. In addition, when women have heterosexual, class, or race privileges, they may unwittingly or knowingly disidentify from women who lack those privileges. Women who have privileges may use "sisterhood" to mask unfair treatment of women who are lower in the hierarchy of a group or organization. Fieldworkers can study how women, in their interactions with each other, reinforce or challenge their subordination as a sex class.

All-Male Settings

Timothy Jon Curry's (1991) study of male college athletes' behaviors in the locker room shows that men don't have to have women present to engage in sexist practices. These athletes talked about women primarily as sex objects and policed each other's sexuality through homophobic remarks. Everything a male athlete does—and how he appears—"runs the risk of gender assessment" (p. 129). Contrary to earlier work that emphasized camaraderie and cohesiveness among male athletes, Curry's study demonstrated that the men constantly competed with each other. Their bond was based largely on their displaying to the team that they were "man enough" to take put-downs by other players. They one-upped each other in their homophobic and sexist comments.

Why did the athletes compete with each other rather than focus only on competing with their opponents? Because no player could count on keeping his particular position on the team. If he got injured or played badly, he could be replaced. This competitiveness eroded friendships rather than produced cohesion. As one athlete said:

> One of the smaller guys on the team was my best friend . . . maybe I just like having a little power over [him] . . . It doesn't matter if the guy is your best friend, you've got to beat him, or else you are sitting there watching. Nobody wants to watch. (Curry, 1991, p. 123)

The players learned to suppress empathy and maintain a pose of invulnerability, thus reinforcing hegemonic masculinity. Similar to the men Sattel studied (1976) in his work on male inexpressiveness, these men had learned to equate self-disclosure with vulnerability. Sharing personal information might also have made it more difficult for male athletes to *want* to compete with teammates.

In the locker room, men reduced women to sexual objects and conquests. On the rare occasion when players spoke of women as people, they did so in whispers. Other players made fun of teammates for engaging in such talk. For example, when an assistant coach entered the room and noticed two players speaking in hushed tones, he said, "You'll have to leave our part of the room. This is where the real men are" (Curry, 1991, p. 128).

Homophobic comments were rampant. Curry (1991) argued that because male athletes are nude in the locker room and physically close during plays, they may go even farther than other men in distancing themselves from any insinuation of homosexuality (which, in U.S. society, associates men with the denigrated category of women/femininity). Despite the equation of men's athletics—and sports, generally—with heterosexual masculinity, some of the men worried that people (particularly other men) would equate close contact among players with same-sex desire. As one coach said:

> We do so much touching that some people think we're queer. In 37 years I've never for sure met a queer [athlete]. At [a certain college] we had a [teammate] that some of the fellows thought was queer. I said "pound on him, beat on him, see what happens." He quit after three days. He never approached anyone anyway. (p. 130)

Feminist fieldworkers can think about the larger lessons men learn from participating in organized athletics (or any other all-male activity). In Curry's study (1991), the men learned to associate hard work and competition only with men; they reinforced ideas embedded in a rape culture through their talk about women as objects to be taken; and they learned to normalize aggression. "Real men" are not nurturant, do not see women as people first, and do not value or seek egalitarian relationships with women.

Curry (1991) surmised that some of the men felt uncomfortable with the culture of the locker room. But not one man publicly questioned others' homophobic and sexist remarks. Doing so would have put his sense of himself as a man—a core valued self—on the line. As the coach's remarks (above) suggest, a man who would take a stand against sexism or heterosexism would also risk physical harm. As we learned in the previous chapter, deviant cases (for example, men who don't follow the norm) put the group norms (masculine "ideals") into relief. Researchers, then, can learn about hegemonic masculinity, and the policing of masculinity, by seeing what happens when men violate others' expectations for them as men.

Excelling in men's sports is an important signifier of heterosexual masculinity. But not all young athletic men try to pursue a professional life in sports, even when they do well at them and identify as straight. Social class comes into play when men—as men—make plans about their future work lives. Messner (1989) interviewed Hispanic and black former athletes from poor and working-class families as well as white former athletes largely from middle-class families. The white middle-class men recognized the slim chance of making a career in professional sports. Even a young man who had been a star athlete in several sports in high school decided not to play organized sports in college:

> I think in my own mind I kind of downgraded the stardom thing. I thought that was small potatoes. And sure, that's nice in high school and all that, but on a broad scale, I didn't think it amounted to all that much. So I decided that my goal is to be a dentist, as soon as I can . . . I'm not going to play basketball forever and I might jeopardize my chances of getting into dental school if I play. (p. 77)

The middle-class white men who enjoyed the advantages of masculinity as athletes in high school shifted their concern to the adult signs of masculinity in our society, namely education and career.

Men from poor and working-class families, on the other hand, clung to the athlete identity, hoping to cash in on it as a pro, or at least to play sports in an arena where they could make a living. They did not have the same educational or career aspirations as the middle-class men, because they knew they had started out with a class handicap and would have fewer options in the future. Messner (1989) relates the poignant story of a man who had been a star athlete in high school but didn't have the grades or the money to go to college. The U.S. Marine Corps offered him the chance to play baseball on their team. Understandably, he accepted. The military sent him to Vietnam; a grenade blew up in his hand and he lost four fingers off his pitching hand. At the time of his interview with Messner, he was driving a bus. Yet, when he looked back, his earlier life decisions still made sense to him:

> . . . I didn't feel like I was gonna go out there and be a computer expert, or something that was gonna make a lot of money. The only thing I could do and live comfortably would be to play sports—just to get a contract— doesn't matter if you play second or third team in the pros, you're gonna make big bucks. That's all I wanted, a confirmed livelihood at the end of my ventures, and the only way I could do it would be through sports. So I tried. It failed, but that's what I tried. (p. 80)

That the middle-class men gave up sports for adult masculine status makes sense. They knew the low odds of making it as a pro. They also knew they would have the middle-class educational resources to succeed outside of sports. In fact, their athletic experiences in high school and college served as resources they could use to network with other men, raise their status with men, and bond with men: Their athletic identity became "a badge of masculinity that [was] *added* to [their] professional status" (Messner, 1989, p. 78). For the athletes from poor backgrounds, athletics was the only hope for a better future and the one context in which they could get the respect that middle-class men could achieve through education and careers. Messner's study alerts fieldworkers to look for the resources class and race provide (or fail to provide) to men in their attempts to live up to hegemonic masculinity, and the consequences of those resources for men's plans and lives.

Men who lack signifiers of hegemonic masculinity—poor men, men of color, gay or bisexual men, men with disabilities—may be especially fearful of the control they are losing or have lost. Fieldworkers can study how men respond to downward mobility in the gender hierarchy. Thomas Gerschick and Adam Miller's (1994) interviews with men with physical disabilities showed that most of the men initially felt their lessened physical abilities to be emasculating. The men used three strategies to deal with their loss of status as men: reformulation, reliance, and rejection.

Men *reformulated* (redefined) what manhood meant, making it fit their reduced capabilities. For example, one man, a quadriplegic who required assistants day and night, said:

> People know from Jump Street that I have my own thing, and I direct my own thing. And if they can't comply with my desire, they won't be around . . . I don't see any reason why people with me can't take instructions and get my life on just as I was having it before, only thing I'm not doing it myself. I direct somebody else to do it. So, therefore, I don't miss out on very much. (Gerschick & Miller, 1994, p. 37)

This interviewee might have seen himself as a failed man. But he found a way to redefine his situation. He could do so successfully because he had the *economic* resources to control others. Hiring strangers as assistants meant, to him, that he was in a privileged position, a boss with employees, rather than someone who had become dependent on others.

That social class is central to such reformulations is illustrated by the experience of another man, a polio survivor and quadriplegic:

> When I say independence can be achieved by acting through other people, I actually mean getting through life, liberty, and the pursuit of happiness while utilizing high-quality and dependable attendant-care services. (Gerschick & Miller, 1994, p. 38)

By controlling others—something middle-class white men are expected to do—both men could reinstate themselves as "real men."

Men with disabilities also used the strategy of *reliance*, holding on to conventional notions of masculinity rather than reformulating them. (The authors found that men often vacillated among the three strategies.) But this strategy was less effective, because others could tell that the men were unable to meet societal expectations for able-bodied men. As a 16-year-old with juvenile rheumatoid arthritis said:

> If I ever have to ask someone for help, it really makes me feel like less of a man. I don't like asking for help at all. You know, like even if I could use some, I'll usually not ask just because I can't, I just hate asking . . . [A man is] fairly self-sufficient in that you can sort of handle just about any situation, in that you can help other people, and that you don't need a lot of help. (Gerschick & Miller, 1994, p. 42)

Some men *rejected* the dominant conception of masculinity, although none did so completely. For example, one man said of fathering:

There's no reason why we [his fiancée and himself] couldn't use artificial insemination or adoption. Parenting doesn't necessarily involve being the male sire. It involves being a good parent . . . Parenting doesn't mean that it's your physical child. It involves responsibility and an emotional role as well. I don't think the link between parenthood is the primary link with sexuality. Maybe in terms of evolutionary purposes, but not in terms of a relationship. (Gerschick & Miller, 1994, p. 48)

Yet even this man, when it came to the issue of a woman working outside the home, said that he could not imagine being dependent on his wife's income. He noted this inconsistency, saying, "That's definitely an element of masculinity, and I guess I am just as influenced by that, as oh, as I guess other people, or as within my definition of masculinity. What do you know? I have been caught" (Gerschick & Miller, 1994, p. 49). Yet there may be cases where a clearer rejection of masculinity occurs, and we should remain open to that.

Fieldworkers should also be on the alert for *compensatory* masculinity—men making up for an inability to signify the dominant form of masculinity. This phenomenon has been found among some gay and bisexual men in their sexual practices. Rafael Diaz (2004) studied the conditions under which gay and bisexual men engage in risky sexual behavior, defined as anal sex without a condom. Instead of assuming that there is a "pathological" group of men who don't use condoms and a "healthy" group of men who do, he asked men when they did, or did not, engage in risky sex. He found that men failed to use a condom when they needed to affirm their physical attractiveness, needed "to restore a wounded sense of masculinity" (p. 378), needed to get rid of feelings of isolation and alienation, or felt the need to escape, at least for a while, "from poverty, racism, interpersonal rejection, and AIDS" (p. 378).

For example, some of the men, from a poor area of San Francisco, visited a higher-status area to look for men with whom to have sex. In this "trip to fantasy island," as Diaz (2004) called it, the men equated the socioeconomically better area with clean, healthy, HIV-negative men—a risky assumption. The men had internalized the idea that the middle class can be equated with cleanliness and health and the poor with dirtiness and disease.

Diaz (2004) points out that the same men used condoms when they felt good about themselves, saw their partner as a human being, and did not cut their mind off from their actions. He argues that the splitting of sexuality from the self is a product of the history of homophobia in the United States, whereby gay sex became something a man did in secrecy, "what you do with strangers in strange places at strange hours" (p. 378). He argues that even those who are out of the closet and living in a gay-friendly city do not necessarily lose internalized homophobia. And because masculinity is tied up with sexual conquest, the men's risky actions could temporarily affirm their physical attractiveness or sexual prowess. Fieldworkers can, as Diaz did, take broader issues (heterosexism, racism, and poverty, for example) into account in examining whether and how men participate in behaviors consistent with heterosexual masculinity (such as risk taking) or in opposition to it.

Compensatory masculinity may also be found among relatively privileged men. One reason men joined the mythopoetic men's movement was to make up for their not being successful careerists (Schwalbe, 1996). The men held such middle-class jobs as teaching and social work, and most were in a two-income household, but they had not made it in the higher-status professions. Although some of the men were sympathetic to (liberal) feminism, they rejected the idea that they were part of a "privileged group" or "oppressor class." (After all, they were kind men who didn't strive to exploit others.) Yet the mythopoetic men were critical of profeminist men. As one man said:

> We have some profeminist guys in the men's center here. They're the kind of guys that if it isn't women, it's the gays. That's probably good. It reminds us that we're this middle-class, white, age-fortyish group. And see, this bothers [the profeminist men]. They say, "Where are the blacks? Where are the gays?" But anyway, the profeminist guys—Bly talks about this; he's got a tape on it; talks about this fairy tale with the dwarfs and how you can't pick up on women's pain. You know all the stuff: the discrimination and all that stuff that's happened to them for thousands of years. We can't pick that up. We can't bear that pain of theirs. It doesn't mean we can't be sympathetic to women, and I *am*. I feel that strongly. And the more we get ourselves together and empowered as men—that's what I see in this mythopoetic stuff. It's a very inward, self-oriented thing. (p. 189)

By focusing "inward," as this man put it, the men insulated their activities in the mythopoetic gatherings from critical analysis. They believed that their rituals and talk could stand outside the public realm and the systems of sexism, racism, and homophobia (of which they were a part). The men felt they were participating in what leaders called the mythological realm, rendering a political analysis irrelevant. These men kept the political separate from the personal, something that feminist women challenged years ago.

The men that Schwalbe studied did not make the kinds of sexist remarks Curry (1991) found in the locker room and that other researchers have found in such male-only settings as fraternities (Martin & Hummer, 1989). But these men still shared an androcentric perspective, taking "men's realities as paramount and [giving] lesser weight to women's realities" (Schwalbe, 1996, p. 193). Their silences, often more than what they did say, revealed their unwillingness to think about how women might look at a situation and why. Here is an illustration from Schwalbe's field notes:

> A man talked about breaking up with his wife. The other men in the circle laughed when he said, "She thinks I'm slimy because I'm attracted to other women. Maybe women aren't attracted to other men." He presented this as if she were unreasonably resentful of his perfectly normal male attraction to other women. But then later in the evening, when the talk turned to "unfinished business," this same guy said, "I have a tendency to overlap relationships. I'll get a new one started before the old one is finished." It wasn't apparent that he saw a connection between his wife's accusation of sliminess and his admitted tendency to "overlap relationships." I thought that if women had been present the connection might have been served up to him. No man in the circle raised this issue. (p. 194)

Similarly, the men did not put down gay men, but when they said they wanted physical closeness with men, they almost always added "but not in a sexual way." This was said often enough to suggest that having sex with men would be a bad thing. And the men who admitted being sexually attracted to other men made it clear that they had not *acted* on that impulse. Thus, the men, in spending time mostly with other heterosexual men, made comments that reinforced androcentrism, sexism, and heterosexism. Fieldworkers should be sensitive to remarks made by straight men, who may appear sympathetic to gay men, that reveal a distance from them at the same time.

Instead of subscribing to feminism, the mythopoetic men bought into essentialism, the idea that men and women are basically different rather than that differences are a product of sticky social constructions, socialization, and the maintenance of male privilege. Without such essentializing, the men could not have worked on revalorizing "man" in the abstract and themselves as men. By claiming that "man" needed validation, they largely denied the systematic oppression of women *as women*. The men kept their energies focused on their inner lives, and failed to link their feelings to patriarchy. Schwalbe's (1996) study alerts fieldworkers to how "gentle men" may reproduce gender inequality, even as they break some of the rules of hegemonic masculinity (by expressing vulnerability to other men, for example).

All-Female Settings

Perhaps it's not so surprising that men in male-only groups engage in sexist practices. But fieldworkers should be aware that women in female-only settings may unwittingly reinforce gender inequality. For example, Matt Ezzell (2004) found in his study of a largely white women's collegiate rugby team that players eschewed feminism and regarded their involvement in this physically tough sport to be about them as special *individuals* rather than about the ability of *women* to transcend stereotypes of female passivity and weakness. These women's unconventional behavior in sport did not offer a radical challenge to images of white, middle-class femininity as a whole.

Rugby is one sport where the equipment and rules for play are identical for women's teams and men's teams, and the women felt proud of playing a "man's game." As one player told Ezzell (2004) in an interview:

> I think rugby is definitely unique in that sense because there is no separation [in the rules], and I love that. I love that about the sport . . . I think some of those rules are really silly, and they're made just, to, um, maintain this proper feminine image. And I think that's wrong. (p. 15)

The women played hard (using no pads or helmets) and believed that players should tough out pain and injuries. Much like the male athletes Curry (1991) studied, the women took on injuries as a badge of honor. One player said:

> Tammie's got a broken shoulder bone—or broken, it was her shoulder blade, all the ligaments were torn; it was basically broken and she played the entire season with it. . . . So she's playing with one arm, tackles this girl that had been talking trash, stands over her and says, "Get up, bitch, I'm not done with you yet!" You know, and when you see somebody do that the whole team is like, "Yeah, let's go!" . . . I mean, there's no way it wasn't hurting Tammie . . . she's going to have permanent damage. And Ella's going to have permanent damage to any number of joints and bones, and she already does. (Ezzell, 2004, p. 16)

The women, however, had a dilemma. To the extent that they were successful at the sport, they became intimidating—and thus less attractive—to men. Almost all team members identified as heterosexual; they worried that the stigma surrounding athletic women, especially those playing a tough male-defined sport, would mark them as lesbians. The women's strategy for dealing with their problem reinforced heterosexism: They made a point of saying that *other* women's rugby teams are filled with lesbians, but not *theirs*. The players at Comp U disidentified from other female rugby players and tried to ensure that their team was "hot"—made up of small, "sexy-fit" women who were recruited largely by members of the *men's* rugby team. Apparently more lesbians had participated on the team in the past, and current members wanted to keep this from happening again. As one player said:

> The years when the girls have been really attractive, like last year the recruiting class, and my year the recruiting class was hot . . . that's when the guys' team is closest to us . . . When [the straight players] felt like the lesbian girls were ruining that for us it got . . . you know, it was like a big point of contention. It was like, they're our guys and you're pissing them off. (Ezzell, 2004, p. 27)

Players cared a lot about not pissing off the men because male rugby players constituted their main dating pool. According to the players, even other athletic men on campus worried about dating presumably tough female rugby players.

In addition to distinguishing their team from other rugby players, the women engaged in identity work that distanced them from women in other sports, women on campus (especially members of sororities), and women in general. They saw themselves as tougher than most women who participated in organized sports, and (hetero) sexier than most female rugby players, though not as sexily "trashy" as sorority sisters—whom they called "sorostitutes." The players effectively "othered" women. They fashioned themselves into the exception—as individuals and as a team. Ezzell's study (2004) suggests that feminist fieldworkers should pay attention to the ways women talk about women outside their group and the consequences of that talk for reinforcing *men's* sexist ideas and labels for women.

Women who play a "man's sport" put the stereotype of women as weak into question. But the rugby players' actions did nothing to enhance the position of women *as a class*. They put down the occasional player who linked women's rugby with feminism as someone "who was trying to prove something." What they left unstated is that players on the men's rugby team would find feminism—and by implication, feminist players—unappealing. Feminist fieldworkers should keep in mind the larger consequences of what women do in same-sex groups. Are they breaking barriers in one way while reinforcing negative images of (other) women?

The female rugby players were not invested in feminism. What happens in women's organizations whose purpose is to lessen gender inequalities?

Alleen Barber's (1995) study of Unity, a women's organization in the business of making sure that corporate women elsewhere are treated fairly, showed that the managers reproduced inequalities—in pay, prestige, and treatment of employees—within their own organization. The managers gave their workers occasional roses rather than bread: flowers on the first day of work, a day off on birthdays, flowers at each 1-year anniversary of work, and free tampons in the bathroom. As one woman said:

> On my first day there was a card and flowers, you know. I got taken out to lunch. And everybody was very friendly. And then I was put in my cubicle and kind of left there. And I realized that people weren't necessarily going to come over and reach out to me, and so I remember the first month or so . . . feeling extremely isolated. (p. 15)

Many of the employees liked the idea of working in a women's organization. But after a while they started to notice that they endured poor pay and bad treatment in order to help women—in other organizations—move up the corporate ladder. Some women even felt embarrassed about getting points from people outside the organization for doing virtuous work. As one woman put it:

> Sometimes I feel guilty because everyone's like, "Oh, you work for a women's organization, you work on women's issues." And I just feel like, "Oh, I'm not really working on those issues, you know? I'm sorry. I'm not. I'm doing something totally different" . . . I guess a part of me wants to be in a more feminist—openly feminist kind of [organization]—and working on issues that I kind of feel are more critical than having women move from managing director to vice president. (Barber, 1995, p. 16)

In addition, when the young women said they felt cared for by the organization, it was other junior-level workers they referred to, not the higher-ups. As one woman said:

> The people I work with are the best thing about Unity. And like whenever there's a problem I can always go to Cynthia or Emily or Marianne [junior people]. And like everybody now, after the phone incident [when a senior person yelled at her in front of her peers]. I mean now I know I can really go to anyone . . . I feel like I can get along with everybody on the junior staff. I mean, I don't have a lot of connections to the senior staff. But everyone on the junior staff. (Barber, 1995, p. 21)

It's important, then, to make sure we know who a woman is referring to when she says she feels cared about by other women. Which "sisterhood" is the participant talking about? Who would she not include and why?

Barber's study (1995) illustrates a more general point that we should think about as we enter all-female settings: Women in positions of power can use "women's culture" as a resource for masking inequalities between themselves and women in subordinate positions. The senior women at Unity counted on a pool of young urban women who would work for the organization because of its (presumed) commitment to women's issues, or because it could provide a stepping-stone to a better job elsewhere. Other young women needed a job fast, and Unity provided one. Barber notes that if the junior women had been working for men, they might have noticed problems in the workplace sooner and attributed them to sexism. It was harder for these young women to see inequalities because the people in power were not only women, but self-defined feminists directing an organization intended to help women. Her study alerts us to the possibility that feminist-sounding organizations may reproduce other inequalities.

Unity was a hierarchically organized workplace. What happens when women of the same age, race, sexual orientation, and class have their own peerlike organization? In his study of a black campus activist organization at a predominantly white university, Ken Kolb (2000) discovered that almost all the participants were women. Yet when there was a public performance, the women always put black men at the center, rendering the women's work invisible. At one major event, a woman had even written the man's speech. In addition, the women lauded the men for their smallest efforts and made excuses for them when they didn't carry through.

Overall, the women were much harder on female participants than they were on male participants. Why? The women felt an obligation to "uplift" black men. They knew that others held negative stereotypes of black men; showcasing a black man in a responsible public position might put that stereotype into question. In addition, the women praised the men because they found them to be among the small group of men on campus—their dating pool—who weren't athletes, who cared about academics, and who had an interest in creating social change. The women, all straight and from middle- and upper-middle-class families, wanted to get involved only with men who fit those criteria. In addition, the women believed that putting men forward might move more people—especially men—to join the organization. As one woman said:

Because sometimes males just have that voice or attitude about them that will get people to listen. If we were to have more males in the organization, I think it would be a bit better and we would get more people. Just like, for example, being in church all my life, people really—they'll listen to women if they come and preach or whatever, but really it's the *male* voice they want to hear. I think if somebody saw, or people on this campus saw, a black male leading something like this organization or just being a leader in any of the committees they'll be inspired to be like, "look at that brother doing this. I should join and see what's going on, if he's so excited and fired up about this." (Kolb, 2000, p. 34)

As others have argued (Brown, 1993; Carbado, 1999; Cole & Guy-Sheftall, 2003; Parker, 1997), only black *men* can serve as the true representatives of "the race"; their achievements are seen as the measure of how well or how badly blacks are doing. (This is analogous to Hochschild's [1989a] idea, discussed earlier, that only men can "do social class" for the family.) The women in this campus activist organization also had accepted the idea that black men should be made central, thus denying the importance of their own work. As Kolb (2000) asks in his conclusion, are there other areas where black middle-class women will be reluctant to criticize black men, including intimate relationships?

When women have crises in their relationships with men, they often talk to other women about what's going on (Oliker, 1989). And women are often supportive. Researchers can ask: What are the consequences of this sisterhood for reinforcing or challenging the behaviors that men engage in and women complain about? Michelle Wolkomir (2004, 2006) studied Christian wives who joined a support group for women whose Christian gay husbands were hoping to become ex-gays. The women experienced sadness, frustration, and rage when they found out their husbands were having affairs with men. It put their identity as Christian wives into question and made it difficult for them to continue to think of their partners as Christian husbands. One woman described the dilemma well:

When Ted was exhibiting masculine qualities in our marriage—taking the lead, taking care of us, working extra hours so we'd be better off, making good decisions, and just being a good family and spiritual leader—I could be a helper/completer for him. God made woman from the man, for the man, for the relationship. I felt like he valued the complement and completeness I brought to him, so I could do my role joyfully . . . The wife submits to her husband as Jesus submitted to God. When the homosexuality came up though, I did not know what to do as a Christian woman. (Wolkomir, 2004, p. 742)

The wives' first strategy was to try to be "better women" by working on their appearance and giving more to their husbands. This strategy failed to change their husbands' desire for men. But the women who led the support groups taught these wives to change their outlook, construing the situation as one that should be "given up to God." Through the program, the women learned to think of their husbands' problem as a psychological illness. Doing so relieved the wives' anxiety about being inadequate women. It also allowed them not to blame themselves for their husbands' attraction to men and to believe that although their husbands desired men *sexually*, they desired their wives *emotionally*. This gave the women hope because it positioned them and their children as their husbands' primary commitment.

The women learned to rely on God—the male headship above their husbands—to make things right, at least when it came to how the women felt about themselves in this situation. As one wife put it: "I've totally let go and let Him take care of it [the marriage]. I feel freed from the worry. It's like, "whatever, Lord. I'm just waiting on you" (Wolkomir, 2004, p. 748).

Yet the women did not sit back and wait for God to take over. Rather, they used their new outlook as a way to bring the men back into line. One woman talked her husband into leaving his lover's apartment by invoking the Bible and God. She told him that there may be ambiguity in the Bible about whether homosexuality is acceptable, but "*nothing*, I mean nothing, in the Bible [makes] adultery okay. Adultery is sin and God hates it. You cannot do this" (Wolkomir, 2004, p. 750). Other wives used biblical passages to convince their husbands not to divorce them. Thus, the women used traditional religion as a resource to keep their husbands around. Their strategies, however, also maintained patriarchal ideas and practices: The husband should be accepted under all circumstances and the wife should obey a masculine God who buttresses that loyalty. The women in the support group came to feel less angry and unhappy by talking to each other and learned how to protect themselves from sexually transmitted diseases. But their beliefs kept them from seriously considering leaving the relationship.

Wolkomir's study provides this lesson for fieldworkers: Women in same-sex groups may teach each other to use patriarchal ideas (submission to husband and God in this case) in ways that both resist their male partners' transgressions *and* reinforce patriarchy and women's place within it. Similarly, Stacey Oliker (1989) found that married women's female friends supported them through marital problems. The kind of support offered by the friends kept the wives committed to their marriages while leaving their husbands off the hook. Husbands sometimes felt threatened by their wives' close friendships with women, expecting the friend to be on the woman's "side." But the men's fears had little basis in reality. When wives talked to female friends about their marital conflicts, these friends usually generated empathy for the husband. As one wife said:

> So much of the time I see only my side—I've got blinders on. And June will say, "You know, he's probably feeling real insecure and angry." And for the first time I'll realize there's another human being mixed up in this, instead of just me and my own passions. (p. 125)

Or the friend might agree that the husband had acted badly, but then point out the husband's good behaviors, implying that the good overrides the bad (Oliker, 1989). One wife said:

> A lot of times, I just looked at the negative. I'd compare Gary to the other husbands. And when you look at someone else's husband, you just see the good side, not the bad one. Jan will point out to me, "You know, Gary helps out with the dishes—or does this or that—and Eddie never does." I'd start to think, "Gee, I really am lucky he does that. He's not all bad." (p. 126)

The emotion work that wives' female friends provided is what Oliker (1989) called "marriage work." The wife's friend acted somewhat like a therapist, allowing the woman to vent her anger. Then she helped the wife reframe the conflict so that the wife could feel better about her husband and the marriage. The friend helped the wife see things from the husband's point of view; that empathy often triggered sympathy.

It's possible for a friend to encourage a woman to act assertively with her husband or to leave the relationship. But Oliker (1989) found that the wives' friends more often suggested accommodative strategies. On the rare occasion when a friend became negative about the husband, the wife turned against the friend. Here are two examples:

> When Carol criticizes Tom for his gambling, I get a little angry: "How dare you? I never say anything about your husband." She just doesn't hold anything back. I don't like it, but I just tell myself she doesn't understand. (p. 134)

> Just before we got married, Marie would listen to my troubles and tell me I probably needed to find someone else. I didn't like that at all. When you complain to people, you really want them to find a solution for you. If they're negative, you start defending him. (p. 135)

Why did the wives and their female friends adopt an accommodative stance? Oliker (1989) argued that for many straight women, especially white women, the wage gap meant that they were dependent on a male part-ner's salary to live decently or well. In addition, the women Oliker inter-viewed (most of her interviewees were over 30) worried about the possibilities of finding someone better. As the main ones responsible for making a marriage work (the "third shift" I referred to earlier), the women thought that they should stay and work on their relationships. They had also internalized the cultural message that children do best if they live with a mother *and* a father.

What were the consequences of this collective marriage work? The mar-riage work women did with their female friends gave advantages to the hus-bands. Sometimes the women resolved a marital problem by talking to a friend; the husband never knew a problem existed. Ultimately, husbands benefited from the network of female friends who helped each other with marital problems. As Oliker (1989) wrote:

> Since marriage work, as I observed it, pressed the wife toward compromise, it solidifies the position of the person who does not need to budge. Since mar-riage work consumes the wife's time and energy and occupies her intelli-gence, the husband's unconsumed resources remain at his disposal (to invest perhaps in social mobility and prestige and further marital power plays) . . . Regardless of its overt intent, the ethic of commitment in women friends' marriage work legitimates men's domestic authority. (pp. 149, 151)

Wives and their female friends, then, do not remain passive in the face of marital problems. But the overall consequence of their "work" is to priv-ilege the men.

***

The concepts "man" and "woman" depend on each other; culturally, one makes no sense without the other. "Man" is the dominant category in U.S. society, so "woman" becomes that which is not man. When men, especially heterosexual men, get together, they may reinforce that dominance, delin-eating their differences from and superiority to women (consciously or unconsciously). This may be done indirectly; the cultural association of "gay man" with effeminacy means that men's heterosexist remarks in the locker room establish that male athletes are *not* like women. In this sense, men's homophobic behaviors become "a weapon of sexism" (Pharr, 1997).

Feminist fieldworkers can remain cognizant of sexist and heterosexist practices in male-only groups. These behaviors may occur in settings in which the group is conventionally marked as hypermasculine (for example, sports) or in which the group is engaged in challenges to hegemonic masculinity (for example, mythopoetic gatherings). In addition, fieldworkers can study men whose masculinity has been challenged (such as men with disabilities), learning how they respond to the loss of privilege.

Women in female-only groups may support each other in ways that inadvertently reinforce male advantage. The "marriage workers" that Oliker (1989) studied made life easier for their husbands, thus leaving inequalities in the marriage intact. The Christian wives married to gay men learned from their female support groups how to live with their husbands despite the men's ongoing affairs. These studies alert fieldworkers to the possibility that supportive relationships among women can maintain the (patriarchal) status quo.

Women who have other privileges (race, class, sexual orientation) may create or maintain hierarchies among women in all-female groups or organizations. If solidarity is expected among women, women with the highest status may use appeals to sisterhood to mask inequalities.

Whether they are studying male-only or female-only groups, feminist researchers can analyze how participants' practices accommodate, work around, resist, or challenge the gender order.

Questions to Ask in the Field or at the Desk

In male-only groups:

- What conception of masculinity do participants share?
- Are members reinforcing hegemonic masculinity?
- What resources for signifying masculinity are available to the men? If some men lack conventional signifiers, how do they compensate (if they do)?
- Do the men take their identity as men for granted, or do they make it a topic of discussion? If they talk about men and masculinity, what rhetorics do they use? Do their understandings of men and masculinity (and women and femininity) reinforce, however subtly, sexist and heterosexist ideas? What are the consequences of the men's ideas about masculinity and men for reinforcing or subverting gender ideologies?

In female-only groups:

- What conception of "woman" or "femininity" do participants share?
- Are women bonding over female-defined activities? Do women use the role that goes along with these activities to retain unequal relations or to challenge them?

- Does being a woman become a topic of conversation, or is it taken for granted?
- Is solidarity among women—based on the identity of "woman"—expected? If so, do higher-status women appeal to solidarity to mask inequalities among members?

***

Doing "compensatory masculinity" or "marriage work" is an emotionally charged process. A man will compensate for the loss of markers of hegemonic masculinity because he feels *threatened* by that loss and wants to gain control. Women who do marriage work empathize with the husband (seeing and feeling things from his perspective) and *sympathize* with the distraught friend. In the next chapter I'll explore the importance of bringing emotions into an analysis of the reproduction of inequality. The sociology of emotions, understood within a feminist framework, can help us understand that the personal is always political.

5. THE PERSONAL IS POLITICAL

In the 1960s, feminists discovered in consciousness-raising groups (Forer, 1978) that the "unique" frustrations and suffering they experienced as partners, wives, lovers, mothers, and workers turned out to be shared by other women. They came to understand their experiences as products of societal arrangements and ideas that reflected patriarchy (and racism, heterosexism, and class inequality). The feminist adage "The personal is political" (see Hanisch, 2006) captured the idea that matters we usually consider personal (relationships with intimate partners, division of household labor, child rearing, sex) are shaped by systemic power relationships in U.S. society.

As I see it, "The personal is political" implies that (a) we cannot understand our beliefs, feelings, and behaviors without putting them into the larger context of oppression and privilege; (b) any action we take—individually or collectively—has consequences for reinforcing or challenging unfair patterns; and (c) "the personal" is not synonymous with "the private," and can be experienced in realms conventionally thought of as public (for example, sexual harassment on the street or at work).

If experience is tied to power relationships, then it's important to pay attention not only to what participants think and do, but also to what they feel. Hochschild's (1983) research on flight attendants and bill collectors set the stage for fieldwork-based research on emotions. She rejected the assumption that emotions are exclusively physiological or psychological states that fall outside the purview of social science. Rather, emotions are fundamentally social (Hochschild, 1983): "Social factors enter not simply before or after but interactively *during* the experience of emotion" (p. 211).

Hochschild came up with the concept of feeling rules: cultural prescriptions for how we're supposed to feel in a particular situation. In symbolic interactionist fashion, she argued that each of us has the capacity to react to and make sense of our feelings. Emotions, then, are not merely "natural" impulses. Rather, we can work on our emotions, trying to create within ourselves the "proper" response to the situation (for example, trying to feel sad at a funeral). Alternatively, we might have the appropriate feeling for the situation, but wish we did not (for example, feel sad when we think we should be angry). We can also practice emotion work on others, trying to induce particular emotional states in them.

Where do gender and inequality come in? Whether engaging in deep acting (what Erving Goffman, 1959, would call a sincere performance) or surface acting (a cynical performance), women are expected to do the bulk of *emotional labor* (working on others' emotions for pay) and *emotion work* (working on others' emotions in interpersonal relationships). Further, women's emotional labor and emotion work are, for the most part, meant to make others feel good—offering sympathy, for instance, even if the other person is not treating them well. Women can break the rules, but not without consequence. Men are largely expected to do the kind of emotional labor that intimidates others or brings them down, such as bill collecting (Hochschild, 1983) and police interrogation (Stenross & Kleinman, 1989).

Women's emotional labor typically requires them to suppress their anger, even at men's sexism on the job. Men's emotional labor typically requires them to repress empathy and sympathy, particularly for women. Thus, "emotional subjectivity can be conditioned in ways that reproduce [gender] inequality" (Schwalbe et al., 2000, p. 436). As feminist fieldworkers, we can, through our observations and interviews, discover the "emotional subjectivity" of participants and analyze how feelings reinforce hierarchy. I'll explore these links in the first part of this chapter.

Most of us want to think of our feelings, especially desires, as indicators of our uniqueness. What could be more personal, more a matter of who we are, than our feelings? But desires are a product of socialization and social control as much as thoughts, behaviors, and ideologies—and thus require interrogation. As feminist fieldworkers, we can also analyze the consequences of desire for reinforcing or challenging inequalities (see Fields, Copp, & Kleinman, 2006). In the second part of this chapter, I'll discuss studies that highlight how systems of oppression and privilege organize our desires and reproduce patriarchy.

Emotional Labor and Emotion Work

The gendered nature of emotional labor and its link to hierarchy are analyzed in Jennifer Pierce's (1995) study of trial lawyers and paralegals. She analyzed feeling rules as well as rules for emotional display. Trial lawyers are expected to display aggression in most aspects of their work. In addition, they learn through training sessions at the National Institute of Trial Advocacy to engage in what Pierce calls "strategic friendliness" (p. 71). Lawyering, then, not only is about cognitive gamesmanship, but involves "highly emotional, dramatic, flamboyant, shocking presentations" designed to "evoke sympathy, distrust, or outrage" (p. 53). The lawyers' language of emotions is gendered and makes it clear that acting unmanly, and thus like a woman, is equivalent to failure. When the lawyers lost a case or didn't "win big," other lawyers referred to them as "having no balls" or as "wimps" (pp. 73–74). Many lawyers' intimidating displays spilled over into their interactions with paralegals and secretaries.

Trial lawyers—especially the male attorneys—expected paralegals to mother them, read their minds, take care of all the details, work overtime, remind them what to do when, and put up with their rants. Paralegals were left on their own to manage their distraught feelings about how the attorneys treated them. As one legal assistant said to Pierce (1995) regarding the male attorney she worked with:

> I feel like I am on the witness stand when I'm talking to him about the trial. After I give him detail after detail to his questions, he says: "Anything else? Anything else?" in this aggressive way. . . . he can't turn off this adversarial style . . . He just persists in cross-examining me. (p. 90)

Another paralegal described a different (male) attorney, much admired by the younger lawyers, as "a shark who ate the people who worked for him alive" (Pierce, 1995, p. 117).

The paralegals also provided reassurance to witnesses, emotional labor that helped the attorneys with their cases. Most of the lawyers were men and most of the paralegals were women. Paralegals' deferential and caretaking emotional labor, and attorneys' adversarial emotional labor, "reproduce[d] gender relations in the law-firm hierarchy" (Pierce, 1995, p. 86).

Fieldworkers can examine what happens when women do not go along with the gendered expectations for emotional display in their profession.

Pierce (1995) found that many female lawyers rejected or modified the adversarial model; 26% reshaped the role, 58% acted aggressively in the courtroom but less so with colleagues and staff (what Pierce called "splitting the role"), and 16% accepted the aggressive model. As one female lawyer said about strategic friendliness:

> I often see my relationship to clients as the creation of a personal relationship. Some would say that's unprofessional. But I really think that relationships based on trust don't emerge from manipulation. I treat clients with respect. I provide them with alternatives and urge them to think for themselves. (p. 122)

Another lawyer spoke of splitting her roles:

> Winning is great, it's important to me. But winning isn't everything.

Meaning?

> Some lawyers turn every encounter into a win-lose situation. In the courtroom, there's one kind of winning. In the office, it means putting someone else down. I think that's lousy. When I'm in the office I try really hard not to be like that—people matter to me. I don't always succeed, but at least I try. (Pierce, 1995, p. 128)

Female lawyers who embraced the masculine model still had to handle emotions that male lawyers could bypass, such as discomfort or outrage over sex discrimination. As one female attorney said:

> All day long, this client avoids my phone calls because he thinks women are incompetents. Hell, it bothers me, but I can't let myself dwell on it, because dwelling on it just depresses me. So I focus on my work. That's what women have to do, work and work hard!

It sounds like you use a lot of energy to keep those feelings beneath the surface.

> To survive I have to *not* think about all these things. If I did I would go crazy. (Pierce, 1995, p. 134)

Female lawyers, regardless of the content of their gender performance, found themselves in a double bind (see Frye, 1983): If they acted aggressively, they could be told they were too aggressive (for a woman); if they failed to act like sharks, male attorneys could accuse them of being bad lawyers. Even a woman's performance of strategic friendliness was delegitimated at times by male attorneys who naturalized it as (merely) "feminine wiles." Male strategic friendliness, on the other hand, was lauded by other men as a clever accomplishment. Fieldworkers should compare how emotional displays are interpreted when they are enacted by women with how they are interpreted when they are enacted by men.

That emotions aren't epiphenomenal but can become part of the labor process is illustrated as well in studies of domestic workers and their relationships with employers. Domestic work, whether it involves a live-in, live-out, or occasional housecleaning arrangement, is not seen as real work by employers and sometimes not even by employees. Because "housework has become fused with the roles of mothers and wives" (Romero, 1992, p. 21), the tasks of cleaning and caring become confused with labors of love (coded as women's work), and are thus not seen as real labor. Also, "housecleaning is typically only visible when it is not performed" or performed badly (Hondagneu-Sotelo, 2001, p. 10), and thus receives little appreciation.

Almost all domestic workers are women, and most employers who handle the employer-employee relationship are women. Even if the employer has a male partner who pays for the domestic service, the wife/mother is usually the one who manages the household—and the domestic worker. This finding signifies that within the household, the domestic worker is seen by the heterosexual couple as an extension of the wife and mother.

The domestic worker often is a stand-in for the mother and is expected to provide care for the children. Domestic workers often value this mothering role, especially if they have left their home country in order to make money to send back to their families (Hondagneu-Sotelo, 2001; Parreñas, 2001). The women miss their children; their ties to their employers' children make them feel valued in their "motherly" role. But these emotional ties to children can also serve as a way for employers to keep domestics emotionally tied to their job, even when employees are unhappy about how their employers treat them.

Feelings of attachment can become an *emotional resource* that both employers and employees use, with varying degrees of success, to control unequal relationships, and fieldworkers should be aware of whether and how these operate. In the case of domestic workers, employers can translate employees' requests for pay raises into an inappropriate way of treating a labor of love. As an employer told Pierrette Hondagneu-Sotelo (2001):

She [the domestic worker] said, "Well, you've never given me a bonus." And I thought, a bonus! I worked all my work years and I never got a bonus from my employer at all. I don't know where she even got that idea! I just felt real bad, and I said, "Gosh, you know, it's apparent that you don't appreciate what you have here. I try to have a nice house for you to live in, and um, I said I never ask you to do something that I wouldn't do myself." You know, again, it goes back to this thing of spoiling these people. But you know, she probably didn't appreciate it or something. So, I made some points. I said, "You know, you say that I didn't give you a bonus, well, why don't you take back all those Christmas presents I gave you and cash them in? There's your bonus!" You know, that kind of thing. I said, you know, "Is money just really all that's important to you?" (p. 120)

Employers who hire nanny-housekeepers want to hire someone who will care about and care for their children, and do not want to think of the work as having much to do with money. In fact, many employers, especially those who have professional jobs outside the home, feel ambivalent about acting as employers and resist seeing themselves that way. Some employers have "liberal guilt"; hiring a domestic worker is too close to the servant-served relationship—and its historical basis in slavery in the United States—for their comfort. One employer said she feared the domestic worker might say to her:

"Well, you are the boss, you know, and you're a hypocrite because you don't believe in bosses and yet here you are, you know, I'm poor and you're able to afford. I have so little and you have a beautiful house and you can afford to rent help and I'm a human being." (Hondagneu-Sotelo, 2001, p. 162)

Employers' guilt sometimes kept them from complaining to their employees about housecleaning that did not meet their standards. Employees knew this—it was one emotion that worked to their advantage, especially if employers expected too much of them. Employers of nanny-housekeepers cared more about the employee's relationship with their children than they cared about the housekeeping. If the domestic worker had a good relationship with the children, employers were willing to overlook imperfect housekeeping or even hire someone else to clean the house every week or two.

Overall, the domestic worker is in a subordinate position, along many dimensions, in relation to her employers. Currently, the domestic is more often than not a woman of color who lacks citizenship and economic resources. In situations where the employer undercuts the domestic's authority with children or fails to recognize that the employee has a life (or should have a life) outside the employer's house, blowups occur. But the domestic worker, unless she has other immediate options for employment, will typically hold her tongue.

Yet Rhacel Salazar Parreñas (2001) found that Filipina domestic workers in Los Angeles and Rome occasionally used emotions *strategically*, trying to make the employer feel guilty, or at least uncomfortable. As one domestic worker said to Parreñas (2001):

> They always want you to be smiling even when you are really tired. They always want you to be smiling. If you are not smiling, they always bug you, ask you what's wrong, if you have a problem. If you're frowning because they said something offensive, they feel guilty and apologize. (pp. 190–191)

Another live-in domestic worker told Parreñas (2001):

> When . . . [my previous employer] would come home, sometimes I would be bawling. I would still continue my work but I would be crying while I did it. I would tell them that I was missing my parents. So, they would take me to the house of a friend. (p. 191)

As fieldworkers, we can become sensitive to which emotions are central to participants' experiences in the setting and how they use their feelings as part of reproducing, working around, or challenging hierarchy. Among domestic workers, finding a sense of dignity and working against loneliness were paramount. Dignity was hard to get because of the low status of the work: Housekeeping is thought of as women's work, dirty work, and even nonwork.

Fieldworkers can ask: What kinds of arrangements make the feeling of dignity possible, even in a work relationship of inequality? Research on domestic workers reveals a system of maternalism (Rollins, 1986; Romero, 1992). As Hondagneu-Sotelo (2001) wrote, "Maternalism is a one-way relationship, defined primarily by the employer's gestures of charity, unsolicited advice, assistance, and gifts" (p. 208). She found in her study of Latina housekeepers and nannies in Los Angeles that the domestic workers did not want a maternalistic system, but instead sought a personalistic relationship with their employers:

> Personalism, by contrast, is a two-way relationship, albeit still asymmetrical. It involves the employer's recognition of the employee as a particular person—the recognition and *consideración* necessary for dignity and respect to be realized. In the absence of fair wages, reasonable hours, and job autonomy, personalism alone is not enough to upgrade domestic work; but conversely, its absence virtually ensures that the job will be experienced as degrading. (p. 208)

In earlier times (see Rollins, 1986), most employers of domestic workers were stay-at-home wives and mothers, and they acted in a maternalistic manner. The professional women-employers studied by Hondagneu-Sotelo (2001) and Parreñas (2001) did not want to have to care (even in a maternalistic way) about those they employed. One might expect that keeping the relationship between employer and employee on an instrumental basis would produce a fairer outcome. But the domestic workers in such arrangements often found themselves lonely and disrespected. One worker told Hondagneu-Sotelo (2001):

> I would arrive in the morning and sometimes she wouldn't greet me until two in the afternoon. . . . I'd be in the kitchen, and she'd walk in but wouldn't say anything. She would ignore me, as if to say, "I'm alone in my house and there's no one else here." Sometimes she wouldn't speak to me the whole day . . . she'd act as if I was a chair, a table, as if her house was supposedly all clean without me being there. (p. 198)

Some employers purposely left the house right after the housecleaner arrived. They didn't want to interact with the domestic worker or have their privacy intruded upon.

The domestic workers Parreñas studied knew that employers could use love as a means of control. As one worker put it, "They love you if they are satisfied with your work, and when they cannot get everything they want from you, they become very dissatisfied" (2001, p. 184). Yet most of the domestic workers Parreñas talked to liked the idea of "being one of the family" and used that phrase to indicate that their employers cared about them. These workers thought of being one of the family as the opposite of receiving inhumane treatment:

Do you like your job?

> Yes. Because my employer right now is a very good employer. They are kindhearted and treat me like one of the family. That is the one thing that is important to me. I want to be treated like a person. Not all employers are good; some are very bad. You can have a high salary but get treated like a slave. I don't care about the high salary as long as I am treated as a person, part of the family, and I get along well with my employer. It is important to have a good rapport and work relationship. What I found among us in Italy, many are unhappy and not content with their employers. (p. 180)

Parreñas (2001) points out that because domestic work is taking place in the home, where emotions and care are expected, being treated as an employee and not one of the family felt like disrespect. In addition, many of the Filipina workers she studied had held middle-class jobs in the Philippines and experienced downward mobility—though higher wages—by moving to Los Angeles and Rome to do domestic work. They had not been treated as nonpersons back home in their professional jobs and wanted their current employers to know that they had higher status elsewhere and thus deserved better treatment than other domestic workers in the United States.

Studies of domestic workers illustrate the emotional complexity of relationships between employers and employees. Because domestic work takes place in the home, an arena associated with women, privacy, and feelings, it is not surprising that inequalities between the employer and employee are accomplished or resisted through emotions. But, as feminist fieldworkers, we should be aware of the place of emotions in other workplaces. That workplaces are meant to be instrumental does not mean that they are, in practice, unemotional. Secretaries in large corporations, for instance, can function as office wives (Kanter, 1977), akin to the role of female paralegals. In addition, treating others in an instrumental fashion is not the opposite of emotionality, but is itself an emotional stance (see Mills & Kleinman, 1988). We can determine which emotions come into play and how employers and employees use emotions in their attempts to get control of the work process. More broadly, we can study emotion work strategies and their consequences.

We can also study the *culture of emotions* (beliefs about feelings, feeling rules, and rules for emotional display, including rituals) as it plays out in the settings we study. Earlier I referred to the solidarity talk ("We're in this together") that masked inequalities between practitioners and staff/volunteers at Renewal. Participants also engaged in rituals that solidified inequalities between the practitioners and staff. Members participated in "circles" at the start of board meetings and at retreats. They sat on the floor, roughly in the shape of a circle, holding hands. With eyes closed, they breathed deeply, focusing on the "energy" that moved from one person to another. After about 5 minutes, participants squeezed each other's hands, smiled, and let go.

A circle symbolizes that there are neither leaders nor followers. Everyone, at least during the circle, is equally valued and contributes to the whole. The breathing techniques created a sense of relaxation, and for some, almost a hypnotic state. This ritual generated a feeling of collective closeness that made it easier to believe that everyone treated each other equally *outside* the ritual.

Staff members at Renewal—those in the lowest-status positions—valued circles the most. When participants arrived quite late for meetings, Jack (chair of the board) sometimes suggested they forgo the circle, but Jane or

Carla (key staff members) would suggest that they have one at the end instead. The circle seemed to provide compensatory value to those who received the least appreciation.

Members also organized retreats, where they dealt with tensions and conflicts. These encounters had the potential to reveal inequalities along the lines of gender and organizational position. But members' folk theories about what causes conflicts and how to resolve them made it difficult to challenge those who held the most prestige and power. Angry feelings, I learned, do not necessarily disturb group solidarity; they can reinforce it. Such reinforcement also keeps inequalities intact. Fieldworkers can attend to all the emotions that members display in the setting and talk about in interviews, and remain open to the possibility that any emotion can play a part in reinforcing or challenging hierarchies.

As I mentioned in an earlier section, participants at Renewal thought of titles, money, and prestige as superficial matters that hid the "true self" and authentic emotions "underneath." If, for example, a staff member were to say "I, as a staff member, resent you, as a practitioner," others could accuse him or her of hiding behind the mask of an organizational role. What happened when a staff member challenged a practitioner's authority? At one retreat, Jane, a key staff member, questioned Sarah's form of therapy. Jane said she had gone to Sarah as a practitioner and didn't feel helped by it (Kleinman, 1996):

> Arthur [facilitator of the retreat] said to Jane, "I don't feel threatened by what Sarah does, do you?" Jane was getting upset, tears were rolling down her cheeks. She said, "Yes, it doesn't fit my perception of reality. It threatens my beliefs. I mean, that you can influence someone by not touching them." She paused for a long while. Then she turned to Sarah [a part-time practitioner] and said, "I'm afraid that I could be influenced by you. I don't want to lose control." . . . After admitting this, Jane seemed to feel better. Jane said, "Sarah, I love you." Sarah said, "Jane, I love you." They hugged. Arthur said, "Look at that. Sarah's therapy works!" Everyone laughed. (p. 77)

Jane's initial challenge to the expertise of a professional in the organization—something that might have made the practitioner vulnerable, at least situationally—concluded with the nonprofessional's admission of vulnerability. Members' "group processing" positioned Jane as someone who had a problem with "losing control" rather than someone who had a legitimate question about Sarah's kind of therapy. Jane knew members' folk theory well and could offer the appropriate response herself.

Members' beliefs were reflected in their language of emotions—their use of "I" rather than "we." Demanding the use of "I" made it difficult for staff to organize resistance or have practitioners take their concerns seriously. For example, Carla (a staff member) came to the start of a practitioner meeting (the only time I observed a staff member do so) and asked the practitioners to up the amount of money they paid to Renewal (construed as rent, but paid for other services as well). The staff had been giving up their salaries to pay for utilities, while the practitioners were paying a small amount of "rent" and receiving much higher salaries, paid directly from clients. Karen, a new practitioner, said:

> "Carla, we think you resent us, we really do." Jack [practitioner] jumped in immediately, saying, "What's this 'we'?" Manny [practitioner] said, "Yeah, I don't like that 'we,' either." Jack said, "Who says that's my issue with Carla? If that's your issue, Karen, then own it." (Kleinman, 1996, p. 78)

Jack's remark about "owning" the issue implied that Karen thought Carla resented her rather than resented practitioners as a group. But Karen thought Carla liked her just fine. Jack and Manny's responses—which carried a lot of weight because they were psychotherapists—silenced Karen. Karen had started off her association with Renewal, like Carla and Jane, as a volunteer, and perhaps that's why she was the only practitioner who had empathy and sympathy for the plight of the staff. She was trying to have practitioners and staff members deal with the discrepancies in pay and other inequities in the organization. Over time, Jack and the other practitioners socialized Karen; she learned not to use "we" to talk about tensions in the organization and certainly not to make statements that acknowledged resentment or anger between unequal groups.

Participants believed that using "we" was unnecessarily protective; it could cover up an individual's negative feelings. And sometimes they were right. But "I" talk could be protective as well—for the *privileged* members of Renewal. Without a "we," there could be no recognition that people received differential treatment based on category membership (staff versus practitioner). And members allowed each other to use "we" if they were building solidarity. For example, at one retreat, Lenny, a practitioner, said:

> "We're all healers." Carla [staff member] replied, "It's important to hear that we're all equal healers. It's important for me to know that. I think that's the basis of Renewal." Lenny said, "Carla, there are times I've talked to you about something and thought about it for days afterwards. You've been my healer. And I'm not just saying it because I know you want to hear it. It's true." Sarah [part-time practitioner] said to Carla, "You've healed me, too. Perhaps we should use the word more, here." Karen [practitioner] said,

"I think it's the whole issue of Renewal, people being unappreciated." A lot of thanking, mostly directed at the staff women, followed. (Kleinman, 1996, p. 80)

This time, Karen's use of "we" was acceptable. As I wrote, "Members rejected the use of 'we' only when someone used it to express a feeling that could have threatened their belief that they were a community of equals" (Kleinman, 1996, p. 80).

However, in organizations committed to participatory democracy, it is possible for group processing involving "mutual and self-criticism" (Rothschild & Whitt, 1986, p. 84) to result in members' challenging their leaders. Joyce Rothschild and Allen Whitt (1986) found that democratic organizations that held such retreats were better able to engage in fair play and avoid blowups. In addition, these sessions kept leaders' influence in check and made it possible for participants to point out potential abuses of power. Unlike Renewal, the organizations Rothschild and Whitt studied were collectivist organizations whose members were invested in egalitarian arrangements; members' valuation of equality led them to create rotating positions and other democratic structures. Fieldworkers, then, should look for instances in which members of an organization or group organize themselves in ways that make equality a real possibility. These may well be groups that recognize that the personal is political and are creating new practices that interrupt the old patterns of inequality.

Desire, Agency, and Resistance

Feminists, like most fieldworkers, probably feel comfortable interrogating those who benefit from unequal arrangements about their desires; we have learned to suspect the interests of the powerful. If we study subordinates—the bulk of what fieldworkers do—we may be tempted to accept participants' desires at face value. Doing so, however, might lead us to miss, for example, what Patti Giuffre and Christine Williams (1994) found in their study of sexual harassment in restaurants: "The sexual 'pleasure' that many women seek out and enjoy [at work] is structured by patriarchal, racist, and heterosexist norms" (p. 399).

The authors studied how female and male servers came to label, or failed to label, particular acts as harassment. Workers' interactions were filled with sexual content; what mattered for labeling any action as harassment were the social characteristics of the worker. For example, white female servers in the restaurants they studied accepted touching, pinching, and sexually explicit talk from white male middle-class servers, but they considered the same behavior sexual harassment when it was initiated by the Hispanic cooks. As one white female server said when an interviewer asked her if she had ever been sexually harassed:

> Yes, but it was not with the people . . . it was not, you know, the people that I work with in the front of the house. It was with the kitchen. There are boundaries or lines that I draw with the people I work with. In the kitchen, the lines are quite different. Plus, it's a Mexican staff. It's a very different attitude. They tend to want to touch you more and, at times, I can put up with a little bit of it but . . . I will give them a hard time too but I won't touch them. I won't touch their butt or anything like that . . . One guy, like, patted me on the butt and I went off. I lost my shit. I went off on him. I said, "No. Bad. Wrong. I can't speak Spanish to you, but you know, this is it." I told the kitchen manager who is a guy and he's not . . . the head kitchen manager is not Hispanic. (Giuffre & Williams, 1994, p. 388)

The server, above, says that the Mexican men have "a different attitude," implying that their culture makes them prone to harassing women. Yet one of the other white female servers recognized that the Hispanic kitchen workers may well have learned these behaviors from observing *white* workers in the restaurant:

> A lot of the guys in the kitchen did not speak English. They would see the waiters hugging on us, kissing us and pinching our rears and stuff. They would try to do it and I couldn't tell them, "No. You don't understand this. It's like we do it because we have a mutual understanding but I'm not comfortable with you doing it." So that was really hard and alot of times what I'd have to do is just sucker punch them in the chest and just use a lot of cuss words and they knew that I was serious. And there again, I felt real weird about that because they're just doing what they see go on everyday. (Giuffre & Williams, 1994, p. 389)

This same server went on to say that white middle-class servers made jokes about sex and "touch[ed] each other constantly," but she had no problems with those behaviors (Giuffre & Williams, 1994, p. 388). Similarly, straight men were troubled by gay men's sexual joking, but not straight men's sexual joking, at the restaurant. As one straight man said:

> There was a baker that we had who was really, really gay. . . . He was very straightforward and blunt. He would tell you, in detail, his sexual experiences and tell you that he wanted to do them with you. . . . I knew he was kidding but he was serious. I mean, if he had a chance he would do these things. (p. 393)

Giuffre and Williams (1994) concluded that current ideas about pleasure "protect the most privileged groups in society from charges of sexual harassment and may be used to oppress and exclude the least powerful groups" (p. 399). In addition, the labeling of sexual harassment was defined by the servers exclusively in terms of individual actions. Female workers, for example, did not consider such on-the-job requirements as wearing seductive outfits or smiling at male customers as instances of sexual harassment. They normalized such mandates as routine parts of the job. Fieldworkers should look for such institutionalized forms of sexual exploitation; these rules send the message that it is natural for men to see and treat women as sex objects at work.

The sexualizing of women in a variety of workplaces reinforces the cultural conflation of "woman" and "sex object," reminiscent of the findings discussed earlier on how male patients treat female physicians and how male blue-collar workers treat female colleagues. Women may enjoy some or most of their sexualized interactions, as Giuffre and Williams (1994) point out. But the *consequence* is reinforcement of the idea that women are sex objects first and foremost.

The female staff members at Renewal enjoyed flirting with the higher-status male practitioners and had sexual-romantic relationships with them. This paved the way for the women to act as the "housewives" of the organization, working for little or no pay and doing emotional labor for the men. As Viviana Zelizer (1989) found in her study of married women's money in the United States from 1870 to 1930, both husbands and wives expected women's "housekeeping income" to be used for the family rather than for the woman of the house. And women in Zelizer's study felt guilty on the rare occasion that they used the "family money" for personal spending. Similarly, members of Renewal accepted the staff women's giving up their wages in order to keep the organization afloat. The sacrificing of their pay meant that they were working only for love, something others expected them to feel good about. And staff members did feel good about their sacrifices, for quite a while. As I pointed out earlier, only after the women's relationships with the male practitioners ended did the women begin to recognize inequalities at work.

As bell hooks (1989, p. 130) has observed, patriarchy is the only system of oppression in which members of the disadvantaged group are meant to *love* their oppressors. As a result, women sometimes engage in practices that win them men's approval but that reinforce inequality for women as a *group*. Put differently, women may be enjoying a kind of *false power* in the setting (Kleinman, Copp, & Sandstrom, 2006). As Sandra Bartky (1991) points out in her discussion of female body rituals (e.g., shaving, dieting, skin care, hair care, makeup wearing), the fashion-beauty complex creates in women a sense of deficiency which only its products can fill or fix. At the same time, one cannot deny the pleasure that women experience in looking good by conventional standards. It's important for us to understand the pleasures of false power, even when such feelings of empowerment depend on painful rituals. And we can also study what happens when women *resist* these practices.

Bartky (1991) argues that the woman who rejects beauty rituals may be threatened "at best with desexualization, and at worst with outright anni-hilation" (p. 77). This strong language makes sense when I think about the responses of straight, middle-class, white women in my undergraduate courses to the suggestion that they resist rituals of femininity or challenge men's sex-ist remarks (see Kleinman, Copp, & Sandstrom, 2006). Most of these female students worry that criticizing men who tell sexist jokes, for instance, will not win them dates. Students are thus invested in identities that stand in the way of their making changes in themselves and in the world. Their self-esteem depends on the approval of others in their reference group, especially the dominant group. Understandably, they don't want to give that up.

The emotion work enjoyed by many women in intimate relationships with men may do more harm than provide women with a false sense of power. Bartky (1991) argues that when emotion work is performed only or mostly by the woman (Hochschild, 1983, 1989a; Rubin, 1983; Sattel, 1976), she may feel good about her skilled work, but is in effect making his feelings more important than her own. In this work of "feeding egos and tending wounds" (Bartky, 1991, p. 99), Bartky finds that:

> . . . the *feeling* of out-flowing personal power so characteristic of the caregiv-ing woman is quite different from the *having* of any actual power in the world. There is no doubt that this sense of personal efficacy provides some compensation for the extra-domestic power women are typically denied: if one cannot be king oneself, being a confidante of kings may be the next best thing. But just as we make a bad bargain in accepting an occasional Valentine in lieu of the sustained attention we deserve, we are ill advised to settle for a mere feeling of power, however heady and intoxicating it may be, in place of the effective power we have every right to exercise in the world. (p. 116)

Bartky is not suggesting that every woman in an intimate relationship with a man experiences false power. Many women recognize and complain about or challenge their male partners' lack of care, and women vary in the amount of emotion work they do in relationships. But her analysis suggests that women may accept men's "confidences" without question when they *do* occur. The male partner who engages in self-disclosure will probably expect unconditional support in return, not a critical analysis: "The exigencies of female tenderness are such as virtually to guarantee the man's absolution by the woman—not on her terms, but on his" (Bartky, 1991, p. 115). After all, women whose husbands talk about their feelings probably feel special ("the confidante of kings").

The woman in the relationship, and her female friends, may consider her lucky to be partnered with someone who is "not like other men," implying that heterosexual men, as a group, rarely offer succor. The "new man" (Messner, 1993), as well as the women he knows, may think he deserves extra credit for being sensitive, regardless of what he confesses. In the cases of extreme unreciprocated caregiving, the woman may come to accept his world as her own, something Bartky (1991) considers "moral damage [incurred] in the doing of emotional labor" (p. 118). Although working on relationships is *human* and ideally humane work (Miller, 1976), it can reflect inequalities when done only by particular groups of people. Who, then, is left to nurture the nurturers?

Some might think that examining the oppressive consequences of desire for the disadvantaged group ignores human agency. This raises the question: What might a feminist approach to agency look like? As fieldworkers, we can examine whether we are accepting the culturally common way of construing agency as "personal choice." As feminist researchers, we can examine where those choices come from as well as what they reinforce. For example, as Schwalbe (2005) asks, if 99% of women in our society shave their legs, can we really call this an individual choice? And if our individual actions affect others, sometimes in unintentionally harmful ways, that too requires analysis. So, instead of asking whether people in a setting have agency, we might ask: What are participants using their agency *for*? And, regardless of people's intentions, what are the consequences of their actions?

Symbolic interactionists assume that agency is a given. Once a child can see herself as an object, she can react to her own thoughts and respond to others (Blumer, 1969; Mead, 1934). This raises questions for fieldworkers: In this setting, what kind of object does she see herself as? And how do others perceive her? In Bernadette Barton's (2002) study of strippers, for example, she found that the women initially derived ego gratification from having men see them as sexually attractive and paying them for it. As one stripper said: "Sometimes you feel like a goddess with all the men looking at you. It makes you feel good. I like being spoiled with attention. Attention you wouldn't get anywhere else. Any woman would" (p. 591). What cultural ideas underlie the strippers' feelings? The dancers have internalized the idea that women fitting conventional standards of beauty is what turns them into "goddesses," or, as another woman put it, "[takes the men's] breath away, whether they're drunk or not" (Barton, 2002, p. 590). Even a drunk man's approval of the woman's body was valuable.

As the strippers discovered all too soon, their male customers were not thinking of them only as beautiful objects, akin to appreciating a painting in a museum. Rather, as Barton (2002) wrote, "On the flip side of male worship lies contempt for women who have stepped outside the bounds of respectable femininity" (p. 591). The woman is not a "goddess," but the "dirty slut in fantasies shaped by madonna-whore dualities and other sexist notions about sexually available women" (p. 591). As one stripper said:

> The job is bad because you have to deal with customers who can be problematic and rude . . . they feel like the normal laws of etiquette that govern any other social or business interaction are suspended there . . . They'll say, "Turn around bitch, I want to see your ass. I'm paying." . . . That's not something you have to contend with systematically in other jobs. (p. 592)

Ego gratification can be short lived. On a given night, men might find the woman unattractive. Such rejection stings:

> But when you're going up to guy after guy, and you're trying to get dances out of them for money, and you get more rejections than you get positive stuff, it can be an ego basher just like it can be an ego pusher. So that's why I think people get tired, is they get tired of being told no. It can be really stressful because you're selling yourself. So it can really wear on you. If it's a bad night, you usually leave pretty pissy, not because of the money, but because you're mad. It's like, what's wrong with me? (Barton, 2002, p. 593)

These strippers learned, as many women have learned who don't strip for a living, that depending on one's attractiveness as a major source of self-worth is a setup for failure. Although the stripper, above, said she left "pretty pissy," she moved quickly from anger at the men to blaming herself ("It's like, what's wrong with me?"). The larger consequence is that men receive the message that women are primarily valued for their attractiveness, and that women are invested in that criterion of self-worth. A double bind for all women operates here: Straight men want women to look attractive and, at the same time, can deprecate women for caring about such presumably trivial concerns as "looks."

The woman who refuses to participate in conventional beauty practices will receive sanctions: "For the heterosexual woman, this may mean the loss of a badly needed intimacy; for both heterosexual women and lesbians, it may well mean the refusal of a decent livelihood" (Bartky, 1991, p. 76). As students on my campus have told me, their counselors for the job fair tell them to wear makeup (though not too much), skirts rather than pantsuits, and so on. Women who wear makeup may think of this ritual as part of their "individuality," and enjoy putting it on and wearing it. But the truly creative fashioning of makeup would likely receive a negative response and thus is quite rare (Bartky, 1991):

> In reality, while cosmetic styles change every decade or so and while some variation in make-up is permitted depending on the occasion, making up the face is, in fact, a highly stylized activity that gives little rein to self-expression. Painting the face is not like painting a picture; at best, it might be described as painting the same picture over and over again with minor variations. Little latitude is permitted in what is considered appropriate make-up for the office and for most social occasions; indeed, the woman who uses cosmetics in a genuinely novel and imaginative way is liable to be seen not as an artist but as an eccentric. (p. 71)

In some subcultures, women have fashioned new standards of attractiveness and new norms for sexual activity that are intended to challenge patriarchal standards. Fieldworkers can analyze how the practices that anchor a group's new identity in unconventional norms of sexual desire sustain, circumvent, or challenge gender inequality.

Amy Wilkins (2004b) found in her fieldwork at a local Goth scene that both women and men were expected to be sexually assertive, hence challenging the usual norms of passive femininity associated with white, middle-class women. In addition, members of this subsociety purposely violated conventional standards for attractiveness: Women wore corsets, short skirts, and fishnet stockings without being called whores, and they did not have to be thin or have a particular shape to be "allowed" to dress in tight clothing. As Wilkins found, the Goths accepted into their scene women who would probably be considered unattractive in other venues for young people.

In addition, the Goths accepted diverse sexualities. Many of the women, though few of the men, identified as bisexual. In addition, some of the straight men challenged gendered norms of appearance, occasionally wearing skirts and makeup. Their clothing was not taken as a marker of homosexuality by group members, and straight and bisexual women found that attire attractive.

The women thought of themselves as independent, sexually assertive, and in charge of their lives and the spaces they hung out in. But, as Wilkins

(2004b) points out, women in this subsociety did not have the option of appearing as anything *but* sexy: "While Goth women may interpret their sexy apparel as 'an empowering statement of female choice,' women in the Goth scene are almost universally mandated to perform a sexualized femininity" (p. 338).

Wilkins (2004b) discovered that the group encouraged both men and women to express their sexuality in multiple relationships. In practice, men had simultaneous relationships with women while women had one main heterosexual relationship, with an occasional lesbian relationship on the side. As one woman said: "There seems to be a double standard—girls in heterosexual relationships can date other women but not other men" (p. 343).

The men, Wilkins (2004b) found, weren't worried about their female partners' relationships with other women; men accurately surmised that the bisexual women in the group remained committed to a central relationship with a man. Some of the men also found it sexy that their female partners were bisexual. As one woman put it, "it's definitely an 'in' thing to be young and bi and poly[amorous] and friendly—to be available" (p. 345). In this setting, then, women's bisexuality was in effect heterosexualized and did not offer a real opportunity for women to develop serious intimate relationships with other women.

Although the women dressed in ways that might be interpreted by men in other places as a come-on, they were not treated this way by Goth men. Or at least not most of the time. As one Goth man said, "I think people unfamiliar with this scene assume that just because some woman is wearing a short vinyl dress and fish nets that she wants to get some from you" (Wilkins, 2004b, p. 337). But Goth women, Wilkins points out, mistakenly equated "the absence of sexual assault" (such as a man grabbing a woman at the club) with "the absence of sexual objectification" and the presence of gender equality in the group. Rather, the club scene was highly sexualized, and women's assertiveness with men made the initiation of sexual relationships easier on male Goths; the men didn't have to worry as much about rejection.

Wilkins (2004b) concludes that when a group focuses exclusively on sexuality as a site for social change—even when it makes women *feel* empowered—the women won't necessarily *become* empowered. First, by making sexuality their only concern regarding inequality, participants might ignore other forms of gender inequality. Second, members do not necessarily share a consistent analysis of the feminist underpinning of their "new" sexual norms, but they might believe that they do, and thus assume they are enlightened. As Wilkins put it, "Participants can use their involvement in transformed sexual relations as evidence of their de facto feminism, shielding themselves and their community from further challenges" (p. 347) to sexism.

Similarly, in my study of Renewal (Kleinman, 1996), I found that members' belief that they were "doing something different" made it harder for them to see their own sexist practices. To participants, working at an "alternative organization" meant that they were progressive. To acknowledge that they did anything that failed to live up to their ideals would have challenged their view of themselves as good people. This realization was too threatening to acknowledge.

Although the Goths valued "sexual diversity," they continued to value an ideology of love and romance. Polyamory (having intimate ties with more than one person) meant that the individual cared about and for each person. Yet it was the *women* who internalized the ideal of romance and did the emotion work in their relationships with men. Because the women valued romance, they tended to give in when their male partner balked if they had sex with other men. That successful romantic relationships were valued by the group led women to accept sexist behaviors from their male partners. Thus, the rhetoric of romance, while experienced as positive, largely disempowered the Goth women.

Dunn's (2002) study of women who had been stalked by men also revealed that the culture of romance, while initially making women feel special, agentic, and empowered, often led to disastrous results. All the women in her sample had been stalked by former male intimates. In the man's pursuit of his former partner, he instilled fear—threatening that he would hurt her if she did not return to him—as well as guilt and romantic feelings. As Dunn wrote, "Even unwanted attention, when it fits within cultural constructions of love, can be interpreted as flattering or romantic. This can occur even when avowals of love are intermingled with surveillance, threats, and violence" (p. 38). Some women were forgiving of their partners because they saw the man as having been controlled by his love for her. For a time, this too made her feel special.

But once the women decided to leave and to seek help from others in protecting themselves, they encountered enormous difficulties when they presented themselves as victims to lawyers in the district attorney's office. In their attempts to get the stalkers to leave them alone, the women often agreed to talk to them. The women hoped to calm the man down and to convince him, often in nice (gendered) ways, to move on with his life. But lawyers interpreted the women's behaviors as *complicity*. The lawyers knew that a case wouldn't be convincing if the woman had had contact with the stalker. At the same time, women who were stalked received so little help from lawyers or the police that their emotion work skills were, ironically, the main resource they possessed. Some women went so far as to return to the relationship, something that appears irrational, but made sense from the point of view of women who had failed to receive help from the outside. One woman explained to Dunn (2002):

> I was scared if I didn't [resume the relationship] that something would happen to me. I felt like he won't—he won't let me go. He's proven that . . . He won't get the message. I don't want him. He will not get on with his life. It was—it was hard to explain. It's hard to explain . . . But the only reason I was with him was because I feared if I didn't then he would hurt me. The police were not protecting me, they didn't get there on time. I felt like that was the only thing I could do to protect myself and my son. (p. 94)

Women had to walk a fine line to show the authorities that they were real victims who needed protection while also demonstrating that they were not wallowing in self-pity. In addition, the woman who aggressively pursued her case with the district attorney's office was seen as too much a survivor—if she were a real victim, how could she be so strong? Bess Rothenberg (2003) also found that women who had been beaten by their male partners but did not fit the "battered woman syndrome" had trouble receiving help from those designated as helpers (p. 783). Women who got angry at their partners did not fit the social type of "innocent" and were seen instead as provoking the man.

Dunn's study, by looking at how "victim" and "survivor" are constructed by those in trouble and those who have the power to help them, offers a feminist, symbolic interactionist illustration of how to incorporate agency into a study. She looks empirically at what the women do—in a threatening situation—and sees that agency is always a part of the story. Whether the woman stays or leaves the relationship, tries to talk the man out of hurting her, calls the police, joins a support group, or seeks legal recourse, she is always doing *something*. Her decisions make sense if one understands the constraints she faces, cultural understandings of heterosexual romance, and the responses of those who might come to her aid. She also changes tactics over time, sometimes changing her self-conception.

The woman who, in our commonsense understandings of agency, exercises the most agency, does not necessarily receive the best response. The lawyers in Dunn's (2002) study resented assertive women who called them day after day to pursue their case. Dunn describes one woman who learned legalese, presumably in order to get the lawyers to take her seriously. Yet the lawyers thought of her as cold; they interpreted her legal knowledge and cool demeanor to signify that she couldn't really be a victim.

As Dunn (2002) wrote, "If 'victim' is a social construction, an identity that is the product of interactions between women and criminal justice system actors, by the same token, so is 'agent'" (p. 184). Those who are hurt by members of the advantaged group still exercise agency. They need to take the role of those in power in order to figure out how to survive. Women who have been battered for a long time by their partners may go numb and walk around in a state they later describe as zombie-like (Mills & Kleinman, 1988). Yet they too are agents. They deaden their ability to feel because they know they are in a bad situation from which they cannot imagine an escape. Giving up, too, is action, even if it leads to a suspension of self-reflexivity.

Feminist researchers need not choose to see women either as victims *or* as agents, but can analyze the constraints of a situation, what a woman feels, thinks, and does, who she interacts with and how, and the consequences of those interactions for maintaining or challenging unequal relationships and inequality as a whole. That the women in the Goth scene, for instance, are exercising agency and desire—refashioning their behaviors and an identity—cannot be denied. What they fashion is part of the analysis. How their actions and identity-making work out in their interactions with male and female Goths, and whether the patterns that unfold point to a reinforcement of patriarchy, a challenge to it, or some combination, is an empirical question. We don't have to deny the oppression of women or the oppressive consequences of desires in order to make women appear as agents, at least not if we recognize that agency should be about *how people enact it* rather than if it exists.

***

The studies in the first part of this chapter illuminate an aspect of work that is rarely found in job descriptions but that feminist fieldworkers should be on the lookout for: emotional labor. Emotions may be categorized as a micro or social psychological concern, but feminist fieldworkers need not accept a false micro-macro dichotomy. Rather, we can show that stratification and social organization do not lie outside what people think and feel but are part of it and cannot be understood without analyzing thoughts and feelings (see Fields, Copp, & Kleinman, 2006). That the personal is political reminds us to analyze the division of emotional labor, emotion work, deference, and intimidation as part of the ongoing accomplishment of hierarchy.

And as the studies in the second part of the chapter suggest, we need to interrogate how members of an oppressed category feel, including their desires, as much as we'd interrogate the desires of the powerful. In empathizing with the oppressed, we might prefer to see their desires as mere "enjoyments" that stand outside patriarchy or even as resistance to it. We need to place their desires into the larger picture, seeing how those desires reflect, reproduce, or challenge the gender order. It's possible that some desires and practices will both challenge and reproduce inequalities. These studies may help us develop a twinge-ometer that picks up on the link between the "personal" feelings participants enjoy—and that we too may enjoy—and power relationships.

Questions to Ask in the Field or at the Desk

- What beliefs or folk theories about emotions do people bring to the setting, and are they shared?
- Who is allowed or expected to display particular emotions or talk about them?
- Which emotions count? Whose emotions count?
- Are particular emotions taboo? How does the taboo benefit some and disadvantage others?
- Do members use emotions, beliefs about emotions, and emotion talk strategically to resist or reinforce inequalities? Do they do so individually or through rituals?
- Are the feeling rules and rules about emotional display among participants different in different situations (in public, in backstage areas, and so forth)?
- What do participants desire? Do subgroups differ in their desires?
- Who is served by participants' enjoyment of particular practices? Are women "trading power for patronage" (Schwalbe et al., 2000, p. 426) by engaging in these practices?

***

Women learned years ago in consciousness-raising groups that becoming self-reflective about common situations and linking the personal to the political could help them make changes in themselves and in the systems that limit them. Patriarchal patterns back then—and now—largely remain invisible and normalized and thus are difficult to unpack. But sexism does not operate on its own. We cannot escape other categories of oppression and privilege, including race, sexual orientation, and class. In the next chapter I focus on feminist fieldwork studies of intersectionality (Crenshaw, 1995).

6. EVERYTHING IS MORE THAN ONE THING

Feminist scholars in the last 30 years have emphasized that sexism is linked to other forms of oppression, such as racism, heterosexism, and class inequality. While still acknowledging that women are oppressed as women, researchers recognize that women may belong to other oppressed groups or privileged categories. As Frye (1992) put it, women share a "common (*but not homogeneous* [italics added]) oppression" (p. 70). How can fieldworkers give empirical weight to the abstraction of intersectionality?

My examination of feminist qualitative studies has revealed two ways that researchers deal with multiple oppressions. Some studies rely on researchers' usual concepts of race, class, and gender; they compare the experiences of women who occupy different social categories (such as race or class), analyzing differences between them with regard to an identity that the women share (for example, mother or activist). In this chapter I'll focus on studies of women. Feminist studies of men use the same method, as we saw in Messner's (1989) comparison of middle-class white and working-class black male athletes.

More recently, feminists have looked at gender, race, and class as "accomplishments" or "performances" (see Bettie, 2003; Wilkins, in press) rather than as attributes of individuals or taken-for-granted social categories. These studies highlight process and practice (Martin, 2003), focusing on participants' understandings and performances of class, gender, and race. They may, for example, examine the ways that people racialize interactions or make class invisible by equating race with class (for example, by construing white as middle-class and black as poor). In this chapter I explore both kinds of studies and what they contribute to our understanding of people as raced, sexed, and classed beings.

Seeing Similarities and Differences

Feminist researchers can analyze similarities and differences between women who share a common identity but differ by race, class, or sexual orientation. For example, Celene Krauss (1993) studied women at the forefront of grassroots organizing in the area of environmental justice. The working-class women in her study shared the identity of activist. She then compared their experiences by race/ethnicity (her sample included white, African-American, and Native American women) to show how "female activist" cannot be understood as an identity that stands apart from a woman's experience of race privilege or oppression.

Krauss (1993) noted that previous researchers and policy makers had thought of grassroots organizers as "particularistic and parochial, failing to go beyond a single issue focus" (p. 248). But she found that women who organized protests against toxic waste in their communities became, or already were, aware of relations of power. Organizing around a single issue brought them a greater awareness of gender, class, and race inequalities.

First she analyzed the *similarities* in the women's experiences of activism around the same issue. All the women developed a political consciousness about the environment through their concerns as mothers. Because of the traditional division of labor in their households, these mothers were in a position to notice environment-related problems, such as multiple miscarriages, birth defects, and cancer. As members of working-class extended families, the women had large networks from which to discover patterns of symptoms. The activists used those same networks to spread the word about environmental dangers. Motherhood became *a motivation and a gendered resource for action*. As one woman said, "If we don't oppose an incinerator, then we're not doing our work as mothers" (Krauss, 1993, p. 252). Fieldworkers, then, can look for the ways that women use so-called traditional roles as motivators and justifications for activist purposes.

The women learned that powerful corporations and the government collaborated in polluting their environment. And they became critical of the mainstream environmental movement, largely run by white middle-class men (Seager, 1993). As one woman put it, "The mainstream groups deal with safe issues. They want to stop incinerators to save the eagle, or they protest trees for the owl. But we say, what about the people?" (Krauss, 1993, p. 253).

Krauss then explored *differences* among these women. The white women had previously thought of "the government" and its representatives as protectors: "I believed if I had a problem I just had to go to the right person in government and he would take care of it" (Krauss, 1993, p. 254). They moved from that perspective to an analysis and critique of the corporate state. As one white woman said:

> We decided to tell our elected officials about the problems of incineration because we didn't think they knew. Surely if they knew that there was a toxic waste dump in our county they would stop it. I was politically naive. I was

real surprised because I live in an area that's like the Bible Belt of the south. Now I think that the God of the United States is really economic development, and that has got to change. (p. 255)

These working-class white women learned about class inequality. They maintained their investment as mothers, but expanded its definition from the private to the public realm. Many of the women described themselves as having been shy; later they became public speakers. They continued to see their role as an extension of motherhood, defending their families in the face of a system that had ultimately led to their children's illnesses or deaths.

The African-American environmental activists, however, did not begin with the same political naïveté as the white women. One black woman said:

When they sited the incinerator for Rahway [New Jersey] I wasn't surprised. All you have to do is look around my community to know that we are a dumping ground for all kinds of urban industrial projects that no one else wants. I knew this was about environmental racism the moment that they proposed the incinerator. (Krauss, 1993, p. 255)

Also unlike the white working-class female activists, African-American women had already worked in the civil rights movement and organized around other issues. Krauss points out that the African-American women's roles in previous movements had been less visible, even if public, than those of black men (consistent with Kolb's 2000 study of black women in a campus activist organization, discussed earlier). Defining motherhood as a role that is public as well as private was not new to black women (Collins, 1990; Higgenbotham, 1993; White, 2001).

Black activists, like their white working-class counterparts, found their concerns different from those of conventional environmental organizations:

This white woman from a [traditional] environmental group asked me to come down to save a park. She said that they had been trying to get black folks involved and that they won't come. I said, "Honey, it's not that they aren't concerned, but when their babies are dying in their arms they don't give a damn about a park." I said, "They want to save their babies. If you can help them save their babies, then in turn they can help you save your park." And she said, "But this is a real immediate problem." And I said, "Well, these people's kids dying is immediate." (Krauss, 1993, p. 256)

The black female activists fit environmental dangers into the frame of racism; the specific problem was similar to the problems they had already faced. They also recognized that members of conventional environmental groups sometimes asked them to join a protest in order to have "black faces" present. The women resented not having been asked to participate from the start. Thus, while white working-class women's consciousness-raising was anchored in class inequalities, the black working-class women extended their understanding of racism.

The Native American activists saw environmental problems in their communities as one of genocide. As one woman who opposed a landfill said:

> Ever since the white man came here they keep pushing us back, taking our lands, pushing us onto reservations. We are down to 3% now and I see this as just another way for them to take our lands, to completely annihilate our races. We see that as racism. (Krauss, 1993, p. 257)

Again, unlike the white women who had an initial trust in "the government" and "the system," the Native American women began with distrust:

> Government did pretty much what we expected them to do. They supported the dump. People here fear the government. They control so many aspects of our life. When I became involved in opposing the garbage landfill, my people told me to be careful. They said they annihilate people like me. (Krauss, 1993, p. 258)

Krauss's study suggests that researchers, in their comparisons of women by race/ethnicity, even within the same class, should be open to finding similarities as well as differences among women. The women's shared investment in being mothers, and the primary caretakers of children, made their awareness of toxins in the environment a turning point in their willingness to get involved. Framing their activism as an extension of their role as mothers legitimated the work in their eyes, and perhaps also to others in the community. Although the role of organizer is public, the rhetoric of good mothering as the ground of participation made that role a "natural" extension of what is usually thought of as private—and acceptable—female behavior. Using a *safely* gendered rhetoric made it easier for the women to participate, and for others, especially male partners and other men, to accept their activism.

Yet the women differed in the content of their transformation of consciousness. The white women went through the biggest shift, moving from a belief in governmental protection to one of critical analysis. Perhaps white privilege made it more difficult for them to see how *class* operated in their lives. This was true despite the fact that they were working-class and thus lacked class privilege. (I will return later to the idea that people in U.S. society often equate whiteness with being middle-class.) And the white women's new awareness, while class-conscious, did not show evidence of an awareness of environmental *racism*. This is understandable; their actions were based largely in a working-class *white* community.

It's also unclear whether the African-American women knew that some working-class *white* communities shared environmental problems. The Native American women, having a history of participation in the public sphere and a belief system that conceives of self, community, and the environment as one, perhaps went through the least transformation.

Differences in race and class can also be used to raise questions about the consequences of differences among women for social change, a key feminist concern. What would happen if these environmental activists came together? Would the white women extend their analysis to include racism? Would the black women and Native American women recognize that white working-class communities also suffer from toxic dumping and thus build solidarity on the basis of class?

An example of *class* differences between women who share the identity of mother is shown in Martha McMahon's (1995) in-depth interviews with white working-class and middle-class mothers, most of whom were straight. Like the women Krauss (1993) studied, these women experienced motherhood as a moral identity, providing them with a sense of themselves as good people (Kleinman, 1996, p. 5). But they experienced the route to motherhood in different ways. The middle-class women thought they had to be "ready" for pregnancy and motherhood. Their idea of readiness was class based: they expected to have accumulated good finances, good jobs (preferably high-paying careers), the right partner, and emotional self-sufficiency. As one woman said, "When I was 35 I found the right Dad. I had [a child] as soon as I thought I had the right father, and that was simultaneous to the marriage" (McMahon, 1995, p. 70).

The women thought of their readiness, especially in emotional maturity, as an achievement. It was not enough to be a woman or grown in years before having children; one also had to be "appropriately adult" (McMahon, 1995, p. 88). In fact, these middle-class women believed that those who had children and lacked these social characteristics were undeserving of motherhood. They did not recognize that their middle-class privileges gave them an edge in having the "appropriate" readiness for becoming a parent.

The working-class women, on the other hand, saw themselves as becoming mature *"through* having a child" (McMahon, 1995, p. 91). The financial readiness the middle-class women anticipated before getting pregnant—accounting in part for their older age, on average, when they had children—was something the working-class women could not count on. As one working-class woman put it:

> [In deciding when to have children] you can't say you wanted to get financially stable, because that never happens, and you'd never have children if you waited for that. It just seemed as good a time as any [to have children]. (p. 101)

In advance of their pregnancies, the working-class women held, on average, a more positive image of motherhood than did the middle-class women. This makes sense; the working-class women had few other options for developing a valued self. The middle-class women had jobs or careers that they valued, and many more of them than the working-class women considered never becoming mothers. As McMahon (1995) explains, the women who considered childlessness and eventually had children were not so much choosing to have a baby and bring up a child; rather, they were choosing *the identity of mother*. The women had internalized the culturally predominant idea that a permanently childless woman is not a real woman and is somehow damaged. McMahon writes:

> . . . [middle-class] women who had earlier thought they would remain childless . . . had [not] taken irrevocable steps in *rejecting* motherhood potential—for example, through sterilization. Whether it was perceived as a desirable option or not, women retained a potential claim to motherhood identity . . . Thus for years women could be nonmothers but potential mothers at the same time. This balancing act made motherhood temporarily a "nonproblem" for both those who "always wanted" children and those who did not . . . The "biological clock" threatened this balance by destroying one side of the equation—the future potential identity and relationship of mother . . . [The women's decision to have children] was more a *rejection* of permanent childlessness than an *embracement* of motherhood. (pp. 64–65)

But not all mothers can appeal to motherhood to convince others that they are morally upstanding people. Krista McQueeney (2006) studied two lesbian- and gay-affirming congregations, one evangelical (predominantly black and working-class) and one liberal Protestant (predominantly white and upper-middle-class). All the lesbians had problems legitimating themselves as Christians. But white lesbian mothers could use the language of motherhood to think of themselves as Christians and extend the traditional family to include lesbian couples. These mothers claimed, with a fair amount of success, that their lives were just like those of white, middle-class, heterosexual families. As one woman in the predominantly white church put it:

> We have a great family. I mean our family is kind of different than everybody else's but I think we have the same struggles, and the same trials, and the same joys that any other family with a four-year-old has. And I think that's how we are seen in the church, as just another family with a young child. (McQueeney, 2006, p. 54)

White lesbian mothers held a privileged position as mothers even in the black church. For example, they regularly gave thanks to God for their children during the ritual of "prayers and praises." This ritual gave lesbian mothers the opportunity to demonstrate that they were good Christian mothers. Yet in 3 years of fieldwork, McQueeney (2006) never observed a black lesbian who participated. Even on Mother's Day, a holiday that supposedly celebrates all mothers, only white women came forward. In church, black lesbian mothers emphasized their identity as mothers only when making public confessions of guilt about being or having been *bad* mothers. As one black lesbian mother in her 30s testified:

> In my early 20s, I found myself a single mother. I never held down a job before, y'all. You know, they say love makes a family, and I think that's really nice, but money holds a family together. And with my boys, I never felt I could raise 'em right, I felt they needed a man in their lives. I love my kids, anyone who knows me will tell you I love my kids more than life itself, but I couldn't shake the feeling that I was a bad mother. So there I was, a single mother, working at Wal-Mart, doing what I could to support them. And you know, I did things I'll always regret. I gave my kids up to family 'cause I thought they could take care of 'em better than I could . . . but when my brother-in-law took me to court, the things he said about me being a bad mother, the people I had influencing my kids . . . you know what I mean, y'all, it's been a struggle. But God worked it out, thank you Jesus! (p. 55)

Both the white and black lesbian mothers challenged the idea that mothers should be heterosexual and thus resisted heteronormativity. But they still reinforced the cultural idea that morally worthy mothers are white and middle-class. Fieldworkers should consider that identities related to women, even those idealized in the culture at large, may be unequally available to or valued for women in different social categories (see Roberts, 1997; Solinger, 2000).

Until Becky Thompson (2004) compared the experiences of straight and lesbian African-American women, Latinas, and white women, researchers had construed eating disorders as white, middle-class, heterosexual phenomena. Her research also challenged the common idea that eating disorders are a product only of the culture of thinness. Although the mass media send the message that being thin is the gold standard to which all women should aspire, Thompson found that poverty, heterosexism, and racism informed the women's experiences of their bodies and of eating.

What did the women share? They had experienced traumas for which eating-related behavior—bingeing, purging, or anorexia—provided a "solution." Contrary to the idea that all women want to be thin to appear sexually attractive, some of the women who had been sexually abused at a young age believed that their "fleshiness" had attracted the abuser. They dieted, sometimes severely, in order to become *less* attractive to men. Regardless of which direction the women went—overeating, purging, or starving—they wanted to become "a size and shape that [did] not seem as vulnerable to sexual assault" (Thompson, 2004, p. 357).

Food became the drug of choice for many women. It is cheaper than other drugs and women could still function well on it. As Yolanda, a poor single mother, said:

> I am here, [in my body] 'cause there is no where else for me to go. Where am I going to go? This is all I got . . . that probably contributes to putting on so much weight 'cause staying in your body, in your home, in yourself, you don't go out. You aren't around other people . . . You hide and as long as you hide you don't have to face . . . nobody can see you eat. You are safe. (Thompson, 2004, p. 358)

Eating provided an anesthetic for the pain of poverty.

Class mobility among the families of Latinas and black women played a part in the women's eating problems. This is clear in the comments of Joselyn, a black woman Thompson (2004) interviewed:

> When my father's business began to bloom and my father was interacting more with white businessmen and seeing how they did business, suddenly thin became important. If you were a truly well-to-do family, then your family was slim and elegant. (p. 360)

Joselyn said that her grandmother admonished her for being fat. The grandmother also made comparisons between Joselyn and her cousins, all of whom were lighter skinned than Joselyn and thus considered more attractive. In Joselyn's mind, being thin could compensate in part for being dark skinned.

Women who identified as lesbians at a young age were most likely to link their eating problems to heterosexism. Similar to other women's problems, bingeing became a way to self-medicate; the women became numb in the face of "inappropriate" sexual feelings and others' potential hostility. Thompson's study, then, shows the usefulness of making comparisons of women across social categories. The comparisons she made allowed her to see that eating disorders are tied to racism, heterosexism, and class inequality.

"Doing" Inequality

Those who study race, class, and gender as process/performance conceptualize these categories as meanings that people use in everyday life to make sense of themselves and others. People treat each other's behavior, appearance, and talk "as if they were indicative of some underlying state" of, for example, maleness or femaleness (West & Fenstermaker, 1995, p. 23).

Anything we do in interaction—or fail to do—can put us at the risk of others' assessment of our sex/race/class (West & Fenstermaker, 1995, p. 24). Most of us "do gender" (and race and class) in expected ways (West & Zimmerman, 1987). If we don't, people can hold us accountable for not conforming to what they perceive as our "true" sex, race, or class. We risk being discredited, for example, as real men or women, or as competent persons.

Cultural signifiers of "true" ethnicity, race, class, and sex are based on a system of inequality. As Candace West and Sarah Fenstermaker (1995) wrote with regard to sex:

> Womanly and manly natures . . . achieve the status of objective properties of social life . . . They are rendered natural, normal characteristics of individuals and, at the same time, furnish the tacit legitimation of the distinctive and unequal fates of women and men within the social order. (p. 22)

A contemporary example is provided by the former president of Harvard in his remarks about why women have not achieved the same success as men. Lawrence Summers (2005) said at a conference that "intrinsic aptitudes" are a major factor in explaining differences in achievement between women and men in science and engineering. However, if we apply West and Fenstermaker's (1995) reasoning, we might say that girls and women are treated as less capable than boys and men in science, regarded as strange if they pursue science, provided fewer opportunities to excel at it, and assumed to be less committed to 80-hour work weeks (expected of scientists) than men. Then, when women "fail" to achieve at science, this fact is treated as proof that women are essentially (genetically) less capable than men. Summers described his remarks as an attempt to "add some provocation to what [he understood] to be basically a social science discussion" (Dillon, 2005). Yet his preferred "explanation" of gender inequality—assigning blame to women as naturally inferior—is hardly a new, provocative idea.

The example of women in science hides the cultural assumption that men-doing-well-in-science is not only gendered, but classed and raced. If we asked college students, perhaps even at a black college, to draw a scientist, they would probably draw someone white as well as male. If asked what social class the scientist came from, they would probably say the middle class.

Another way of saying that people "do" gender, race, and class is that we *perform* these categories. In feminist fieldwork studies, however, performance does not imply that individual agency (a virtuoso performance) is all that matters. We look for the ways that these performances are culturally scripted as well as improvised. Do these scripts, when enacted, largely reproduce or challenge sex, race, and class inequalities? As Julie Bettie (2003) found in her ethnography of working-class and middle-class white and Mexican-American girls in their senior year of high school:

> Structural, institutionalized inequalities preexist and for the most part produce girls' race-class-gender performances. While these structures are not automatically or inevitably *re*produced, but rather are constantly constituted and historically contingent, by and large structures of inequality reappear over time, albeit with new veneer. With few exceptions, it appeared that working-class girls would have working-class futures, and middle-class girls, middle-class futures. (p. 192)

Bettie's (2003) study shows that we can't fully understand the reproduction of inequality through performance without also paying attention to what is *absent* from participants' discourse. For example, class differences among the students she studied remained obscure; students interpreted each other's behaviors/performances largely as markers of race and sex. When a Filipina-American student told Bettie, "There's a lot of trashing of white girls really, and Mexican girls who act white" (p. 84), Bettie asked what she meant by acting white. The student answered, without hesitation, that she was referring to "the preps" (college-bound, middle-class girls). Bettie then used colloquial terms for categories of students (smokers, hicks) who came from low-income white families to see whether the same student thought of whiteness as something distinguished from class:

Julie [Bettie]:   Not the smokers or the hicks or—

Erica: Oh, no, never smokers, basically the preps. (p. 84)

Erica, like many other students, conflated race with class. The preps were white middle-class college-bound students, and in that setting, everyone assumed that acting white meant emulating middle-class white behaviors, not working-class white behaviors.

The absence of a recognition of class—culturally widespread in the United States—made it difficult for the Mexican-American girls to understand how white students could be anything other than successful. As one student said to Bettie (2003): "I mean, they're white, they've had the opportunity. What's wrong with them?" (p. 85). Fieldworkers can consider how such statements (and beliefs) make it difficult to build working-class solidarity across ethnic and racial groups.

Bettie points out that Mexican-American middle-class students were more accepting of Mexican-American working-class students than white middle-class students were of white working-class students. The Mexican-American preps called upon racism to explain the difficulties of some of the working-class members of their racial group. But the white preps distanced themselves from white working-class students, seeing themselves as better people than their hard-living counterparts. When the white preps did offer compassion, they tended to refer to broken homes or bad parents as the cause of the students' misbehaviors at school. The preps called upon pop cultural ideas about "family problems" as the original cause of young poor people's problems, even when it made little sense to do so. For instance, when two white middle-class students said that divorced parents accounted for the white hard-livers' lack of success at school, Bettie (2003, p. 118) pointed out that both girls were also from divorced families.

The white preps' accounts offer an image of themselves as somewhat compassionate; after all, they aren't blaming their peers, but their peers' parents. At the same time, the preps' accounts are individualistic and hide the fact that poverty and discrimination are at work. This is not surprising in a society where class is treated as either nonexistent or a result of a natural distribution of talent and hard work.

Bettie (2003) alerts researchers to the importance of *gender strategies* in studying the performance of raced and classed identities. The working-class girls—Mexican-American and white—differentiated themselves from the preps. Bettie argues that their gender strategies compensated for their lack of opportunities to do well in school and beyond:

> They created styles and practices that worked as alternative badges of dignity; they made overt claims to adult status [such as getting pregnant, bringing up children]; and they invoked various kinds of claims to authenticity (racial, subcultural) as a strategy to heal various injuries of inequality. (p. 167)

Those very strategies, however, made it more difficult for working-class and poor girls to escape from class inequalities and racism. They became invested in being "cool." The performance of "cool" included missing class, not knowing which assignments were due when, attending class stoned, or not doing well. As Bettie (2003) put it, the students' displays of indifference communicated this message: "I cannot fail at your game if I opt out of it" (p. 108).

The Mexican-American poor girls performed, through their clothing and makeup, the kind of sexualized selves that led others, including teachers, to see them as promiscuous and predominantly oriented toward heterosexual romance. Bettie was unconvinced that this group of students was more sexually active than others, including the preps. But the hard-living Mexican-American girls were less likely to have abortions and more likely to keep their babies than other students. This visible display made it easier for others to equate sexually suspect female behavior with poor Mexican-American girls. Bettie also points out that the poorer girls were quite cynical about men and expected to have financial independence. Here is an excerpt from Bettie's (2003) field notes:

Leticia: Them boys who want to date us are buggin.' They try to control you and tell you what to do.

Lorena: Like Omar. We were standing by the business building one day, and he hands me his coat and says, "Watch this." Then he goes off with some friends. I just left the coat on the bench. When he saw me, he said, "Why didn't you watch my coat? It coulda got stolen." Man, that ain't my job!

Yolanda: And they tell you you shouldn't wear certain things.

Lorena: Yah, like that white top I had on yesterday. Miguel said I shouldn't wear that. I look like a hoochie [laughing]. I told him *he* looked stupid, like Columbus. (p. 73)

As Bettie (2003) wrote, las chicas "brought heterosexual romance and girl culture into the classroom as a favorite form of distraction" (p. 59); they weren't more interested in romance than the preps. But others took their style as indicative of "promiscuity." Such labeling had real effects— teachers took these girls less seriously.

A focus on performance can lead researchers to attend to participants who don't "do" race, sex, or class in culturally appropriate ways. How do others react when they challenge the usual expectations for performance? Wilkins (2004a) studied Puerto Rican wannabes—white, largely middle-class young women who dress and act in ways that violate expectations of proper white middle-class femininity. In Wilkins's words:

> The stereotypical Puerto Rican wannabe rejects white middle-class cultural style, adopting an urban presentation of self associated with people of color. She wears hip-hop clothes and Puerto Rican hairstyles, drinks malt liquor, and smokes Newports. She adopts an attitude, acting tough and engaging in verbal and physical fights. And perhaps most important, she dates and has sex with black and Puerto Rican men. (p. 104)

The wannabe crosses race and class lines, but blacks and Puerto Ricans reject her claims to authenticity. At the same time, whites find her too loud and aggressive or to have fallen from (white, middle-class) grace, a victim of exploitation by black or Puerto Rican men. As one white woman explained, wannabes are "seen as more sexual than other *white* girls. They're more open—they talk about it. They're proud . . . They seem like *typical* boys—sex is an accomplishment" (Wilkins, 2004a, p. 110). Another white woman said, "They let guys talk them into whatever they want them to do" (p. 110). The white nonwannabes alternate between rhetorics of victimization and blame, all the while making it clear that they—unlike the wannabes—will be neither victims nor blameworthy.

Most of the wannabes, like the high school girls Bettie (2003) studied, did not recognize social class. Yet the wannabes' interest in crossing over to another racial group was class-related. These women showed no interest in middle-class black or Puerto Rican men. Their attraction to men of color was informed by stereotyping of poor and working-class men—especially black and Puerto Rican poor men—as tough.

Wilkins's (2004a) study directs researchers to look for the ways that participants use sexuality to police boundaries around class, race, and sex. By dating black and Puerto Rican men, the wannabes reinforced the divide between good (white middle-class) girls and bad (nonwhite poor) girls. Some white men were attracted to the wannabes, seeing them as somewhat exotic for their racial transgression and "badness." The men positioned themselves as the white (middle-class) knights who were trying to save these formerly good girls—by having sex with them.

And black and Puerto Rican men at times did not take the wannabes seriously as long-term partners. By saying that they saw the wannabes only as sex objects, the men could justify their liaisons with wannabes to black and Puerto Rican women who resented the men for dating white women.

Unlike the young women in Bettie's (2003) study, the wannabes were genuinely interested in long-term romance (with black and Puerto Rican men), and rarely found it. As Wilkins (in press) discovered in her larger study of Goths, wannabes, and women in Campus Crusade for Christ, the women's privileging of heterosexual romance led them to put up with men's mistreatment or set aside their own career goals. It also led the women to value romance with men over friendships with women, in turn making these young women more dependent on men. Thus, their performances ultimately reinforced their vulnerability as women and gender inequality overall.

The example of the wannabes demonstrates that women's performances have *material* consequences and these should be examined along with analyses of identity. The committed wannabes experienced downward mobility. Most of them had children and became single mothers with low-paying jobs or depended on meager public assistance. And these very consequences were resented by women of color who saw the wannabes as reinforcing stereotypes of black and Puerto Rican women as sexually loose welfare queens.

Boys' performances of masculinity can also have consequences for their class futures, and these, too, should be examined. Ann Arnett Ferguson (2001) studied a school in which one quarter of the students were black boys. Yet in 1991–1992, black boys accounted for half of the students who were sent to the "Punishing Room" and four fifths of the boys who were suspended. Teachers and administrators at Rosa Parks School used essentialized notions about race and gender in their treatment of students, especially when it came to punishments. The adults in the setting, including some African-American teachers, *equated* bad behavior with African-American boys. In addition, they tended to "adultify" (p. 80) black boys, seeing their misbehaviors as portents of bad (adult) futures. As Ferguson (2001) recalled from the early days of her fieldwork:

> . . . one of the adults, an African American man, pointed to a black boy who walked by us in the hallway. "That one has a jail-cell with his name on it," he told me. We were looking at a ten-year-old, barely four feet tall, whose frail body was shrouded in baggy pants and a hooded sweatshirt. The boy,

Lamar, passed with the careful tread of someone who was in no hurry to get where he was going. He was on his way to the Punishing Room. (p. 1)

Although teachers thought of misbehaviors as gendered ("Boys will be boys"), they made a distinction between white boys and black boys. White boys could be Good Bad Boys, naughty rather than vicious. This became clear in the remarks of one white teacher as she described an ideal male student, a white boy:

He's not really Goody Two-shoes, you know. He's not quiet and perfect. He'll take risks. He'll say the wrong answer. He'll fool around and have to be reprimanded in class. There's a nice balance to him. (p. 91)

This teacher, like other teachers at the school, made it possible for white boys to live up to conventional standards of masculinity among peers without being seriously punished. But this option was rarely open to black boys. They had to choose between being conformists in school—something that challenged their masculinity among peers—and engaging in misbehaviors that, because of racialized and gendered ideas about deviance, would probably lead them to the Punishing Room.

The boys knew quite well how teachers perceived them, and many opted to act in hypermasculine ways. Going to the Punishing Room became a badge of honor and they performed "badness" for their peers. As one boy told Ferguson (2001):

The teacher says [he mimics a high-pitched fussy voice], "you not the teacher of this class." And then I say [adopts a sprightly cheeky tone], "Oh, yes I am." Then she say, "No, you're not, and if you got a problem you can just leave." I say, "Okay" and leave. (p. 177)

The black boys' behaviors made major challenges to their teachers' authority. Ferguson points out that for the black boys, making subtle challenges would not have gone over well with peers. Given racist and gendered understandings of black masculinity, the black boy who wanted to get points for performing masculinity had to do so flagrantly. As one of the student specialists at the school told Ferguson (2001), "The white kids are sneaky, the black kids are more open" (p. 178). The black boys' "open" performances tapped into the teachers' assumption that troublemaking is inherent in black boys and thus requires major punishments. These punishments became resources used by the black boys in their dramatic performances, in turn providing "proof" of their masculinity to peers and of their (racialized) "bad attitude" to teachers. Ferguson's study sensitizes us to the self-fulfilling prophecy of racism that may operate in the settings we study: Teachers' differential treatment of black boys, along with gendered ideas about black boys and men, reproduced the very behaviors that the teachers disliked.

Many of the boys misbehaved by sexually harassing girls. Again, black boys' inappropriate behaviors were taken much more seriously than those of white boys. This was especially true when black boys directed their harassment at white middle-class girls. The teachers, however, saw themselves as race-blind, treating all the children the same way when it came to punishments. As in many settings, race (and racism) formed an "absent presence" (Apple, 1999, p. 12).

An example of how racism and sexism inform interaction in ways that remain hidden to participants and difficult for researchers to uncover is found in Jessica Fields's (2005) study of debates over sexuality education in a predominantly black county of North Carolina. She shows that advocates of abstinence-only programs *and* advocates of abstinence-plus programs used race-neutral rhetorics that relied on racist and sexist assumptions. Both parties claimed that they were merely doing "what was best for the children" while reinforcing images of black girls as sexually corruptible by black men and adultified black boys. White girls (and to some extent white boys) were perceived as those who would be "infected" with the bad behaviors of black boys and black girls.

Children are supposedly thought of as innocent, but Fields (2005) and Ferguson (2001) point out that this idea is white, middle-class, and suburban. Those who espoused the abstinence-only position claimed a 20–60–20 divide to make their claims. Although the statistic comes from nowhere, they said that about 20% of the children are a lost cause—they will engage in bad behaviors no matter what adults do to change them. Another 20% are the best children, who will do the right thing regardless of what adults teach them. That leaves 60% who could go either way and, if given "too much" information about sex, might mess up.

Although the bad 20% were never named, the fact that Southern County was largely African-American and poor meant that "everyone knew" who that number referred to. In a dramatic moment at a board meeting, a white fifth-grade girl, brought by her mother, said, "I don't think you should tell me how to use condoms" (Fields, 2005, p. 561). Whether or not she intended it so, her statement became a performance of white, middle-class, virginal femininity— which should be protected from boys and especially poor black boy-men.

Advocates of abstinence plus (comprehensive sexuality education) "turned the Southern County debate away from continued vilification and toward compassion" (Fields, 2005, p. 563). They argued that educators should care about all children and not just the 60%. Using the language of children-having-children, they argued that teen pregnancy was a problem because it closed off childhood.

But abstinence-plus advocates used rhetorics that rested on the assumption of the "bad" (black) family. If children were having children, they argued, it was because the teens had not been parented adequately, particularly by their mothers. As one white married mother told Fields (2005) in an interview:

> I can pick out girls in her [the daughter's] class who are going to be pregnant before they graduate from high school. . . . They dress suggestively. They are mature beyond their years. They know more information because they have seen it. Granted, my daughter knows about [sex], but she is still very innocent. I can pick out three in her class right now. Their mothers are out there having children with different fathers. (p. 565)

This mother did not say anything about race, speaking as if she were describing any girl or any mother. But in a school that is predominantly black, in a county that is largely black and poor, in a society in which childhood innocence is coded as white, her comments were clear. In addition, abstinence-plus advocates reinforced the view of (black) men as predatory, and black girls' mothers as those who allowed (black) men to prey on their daughters. As one woman said, "I'm talking about mothers who allow men to come into their homes and impregnate their children" (Fields, 2005, p. 566).

As Fields (2005) points out, sexuality education was not targeted at "children," but at girls, especially African-American girls, who were seen either as a corrupting influence on white girls or as victims of (black) boymen. Young women, especially African-American young women, could be either "hypersexual or asexual—voracious women or chaste children" (Fields, 2005, p. 568). There was no room for healthy sexuality for girls (and women) in these debates about sexuality education, especially if they were black. Fields's study, like Bettie's (2003), demonstrates that people bring race, class, gender, and sexuality into interactions in hidden ways. Researchers must uncover these codes and analyze how people use them to reproduce inequalities.

***

The studies in the first part of this chapter offered comparisons among women along the dimensions of race, class, and sexuality (to name three that are key). Comparing groups of women sensitizes us to differences in how women respond to common problems. For example, it is difficult for any woman to escape the mandate to be attractive, and images that are largely white, heterosexual, and middle-class dominate the media. But women react differently to those images, and to messages from parents, friends, and others, depending on their social class, race, and sexual orientation. Feminists can also study how women of different races, classes, and sexual orientations use traditional roles (such as motherhood) as gendered resources to resist patriarchal expectations, even as those very resources also reinforce conventional gender expectations.

To undertake the kind of studies discussed in the second half of this chapter, fieldworkers tune in to how people understand each other in relation to cultural ideas about sex, race, and class, among other categories. As West and Fenstermaker (1995) point out, these categories coalesce. The wannabe, for example, is acting inappropriately not only for her race, but also for her sex and class. A young, white, middle-class woman is not supposed to desire a poor black man sexually—and certainly not as a long-term partner. She is also not supposed to have unprotected sex with black men, and if she gets pregnant, she is not supposed to keep the child. The wannabes do all of the above.

This approach makes us aware of process, examining how people racialize interactions or understand what is going on as a matter of sex or class. And as Bettie (2003), Ferguson (2001), and Fields (2005) make clear, we need to pay attention to what may be less than obvious. Beliefs about race or class might remain hidden from participants—and from us—while still informing interactions and having consequences. Age, ability, and other categories may also work invisibly, and it's our job to make all of these social dimensions visible.

Questions to Ask in the Field or at the Desk

Studies on similarities and differences:

- What do members of the same sex share (for example, are they mothers, activists, athletes)?
- Do they see their identity in the same way? In different ways?
- How does the race, class, or sexual orientation of the women (or men) inform their different understandings of their shared identity?

- Are the women (or men) who share an identity aware that women (or men) of other classes, races, or sexual orientations also have that identity? Do they identify with them? Do they generalize their understandings about their role (intentionally or not) only to their own race, class, or sexual orientation?
- Do they interact with others who share that identity but differ by race, class, or sexual orientation?
- What categories other than race, class, and sexual orientation (such as age or ability) might be relevant for comparison?

Studies on "doing gender":

- Do participants make universalizing comments (such as, "We need to save the children") that hide who they are really talking about (poor people, people of color, etc.)? If so, what are the indicators that such comments are classed or raced? Do they, for instance, refer to "those people," or use other derogatory language at times that slips from their usual benign-sounding rhetoric of general categories?
- What does universalizing language accomplish? Who does it serve and how?
- Do participants talk about class, or does it remain hidden? Does racialized language work as a substitute for referring to class, or as a way of putting class and race together (for example, does black become a synonym for lower class or poor, erasing the existence of poor whites)?
- Do women/girls in other oppressed categories use sexual strategies as a way of responding to heterosexism, racism, and class inequality as women? If so, what are the consequences of those strategies for reinforcing or challenging sexism, racism, and class inequality?
- If men/boys are members of other oppressed categories, do they respond in "masculine" ways that reinforce racial, class, or sexual oppression?
- How are participants' performances of race/class/gender culturally scripted as well as improvised? Do these performances largely reproduce or challenge inequalities?
- If girls/women or boys/men act in inappropriate ways for their race or class, how do others (those in their own groups or outsiders) respond? Do the girls/women or boys/men justify their actions?

***

The studies in this chapter show that sexism, racism, class inequality, and heterosexism are intertwined. And people live out these patterns in everyday life, doing what feels "natural." In the case of sexism, gender expectations may be "fluid and shifting," but the part they play in reproducing inequality remains "robust and persisting" (Martin, 2003, p. 344). How, as feminists, may we use our insights from these studies to reduce inequalities? I turn to a discussion of that question in the final chapter.

7. BRINGING IT HOME

> Feminist consciousness is both consciousness of weakness and consciousness of strength . . . it leads to the search both for ways of overcoming those weaknesses in ourselves which support the system and for direct forms of struggle against the system itself.
>
> —Sandra Bartky,
> *Femininity and Domination*

It's not fashionable today for women to speak of weaknesses in themselves or of a system that victimizes. I've learned this lesson from teaching courses in fieldwork, the sociology of gender, and social and economic justice to undergraduates and graduate students for many years. Most of the (straight, white, middle-class) women in my classes are initially skeptical about Frye's (1983) "birdcage" image of women's oppression. Perhaps a birdcage of racism exists, many of them say, but surely the days of sexism are over. Others concede that a birdcage of sexism is a possibility, but believe that *they* have managed to stay out of it (see Kleinman, Copp, & Sandstrom, 2006).

The privileges of race, class, and sexuality shared by these students have cushioned some of the effects of living in a sexist society. In addition, the mainstream media have successfully mocked and vilified feminists while denying or trivializing sexism. So it's not surprising that female students first experience the idea of sexism as "victimizing." They blame the bearers of the bad news, as if sexism might disappear if only we'd shut up about it. Even the students who call themselves feminists are likely to believe that sexism is no longer much of a problem. They share an understanding of feminism put forward by Jennifer Baumgardner and Amy Richards (2003): "Feminism isn't about what choice you make, but the freedom to make that choice" (p. 450). According to this view, whatever we do is OK, as long as we call it feminist. Saying one is a self-identified feminist presumably

confers virtue. But the identity of feminist, or any other progressive identity, is no guarantee that a person's choices are good ones. And the danger
is that "feminist" becomes an identity that absolves its occupant of any critical self-reflection.

By the end of my courses, most of the students recognize not only
the existence of systematic gender inequalities but the ways that they have
reinforced—and can now challenge—those inequalities in their everyday
lives. As students become aware of the "wires" of the birdcage and the
complex connections among the wires, they experience growing pains. But
they also develop "a joyous consciousness of [their] own power" and "the
possibility of unprecedented personal growth" (Bartky, 1991, p. 16).

What does this mean for conducting feminist field studies? The research
we do will reflect the kind of feminism we practice and our awareness of
where we are in our feminist journey. In the introduction to this book, I laid
out the feminist assumptions that inform my work and some of the authors
who have influenced my thinking. I occasionally reread their work to bring
me back to what I consider the basics of feminism. And the basics include
a recognition of the systematic nature of sexism and other inequalities, the
adaptability of patriarchy, and the ability of human beings to reinforce or
subvert that system.

If we fail to see how we participate, in large and small ways, in the reproduction of inequalities, then we are likely to come up with self-justifications
that will carry over into our analysis of what's going on in the field (see
Kleinman & Copp, 1993). Feminist fieldwork analysis, then, requires hon-
esty about our own lives within patriarchy, including our emotions. We can
ask ourselves: Are we enjoying oppressive desires, rituals, and actions? Are
we reinforcing racism or class inequality in our relations with others? As
Hochschild (1983) wrote, a feeling is a "sense, like the sense of hearing or
sight . . . We experience it when bodily sensations are joined with what we
see or imagine . . . From feeling we discover our own viewpoint on the
world" (p. 17). We need to know what that viewpoint is if we're going to do
good work.

Our "outlaw emotions" (Jaggar, 1989) or twinge-ometer might tell us
that inequality is present in a setting. But we shouldn't assume that our feelings are accurate. Rather, we need to put them to empirical tests. Feelings
are a resource, not the final word. According to Jaggar (1989), an uncriti-
cal feeling should not

> . . . be substituted for supposedly dispassionate investigation. . . . Like all our
> faculties, they may be misleading, and their data, like all data, are always

subject to reinterpretation and revision. Because emotions are not presocial, physiological responses to unequivocal situations, they are open to challenge on various grounds. They may be dishonest or self-deceptive, they may incorporate inaccurate or partial perceptions, or they may be constituted by oppressive values. (p. 163)

A feminist analysis also includes the ways we have found to "adapt to, reject, resist, or avoid" patriarchal patterns (Frye, 1992, p. 67). We don't have to become perfect feminists, an impossibility. Rather, it means that we know where we are at the moment, do the best we can, and hope to do better in the future. But we try *not* to fool ourselves into believing that our unfeminist feelings and actions are OK.

I learned to watch out for the potentially harmful consequences of a moral identity—one that gives us a sense of ourselves as good people—at Renewal. I came to the conclusion there that participants failed to see how they reproduced inequalities because it was too painful for them to do so. Their moral identity ("alternative") was so highly valued that they could not bear to believe they had failed to live up to their own standards and had violated some of their ideals. Their investment in an alternative identity stood in the way of critical self- and group reflection.

Baumgardner and Richards's feminism-as-choice comes pretty close to the largely apolitical ideas held by members of Renewal. Both share an individualistic belief system that disregards the interconnectedness of human beings and the consequences of our actions on others. Individualism leaves privileges intact by ignoring the fact that not everyone has the resources to do whatever they desire or the power to make things happen. It also ignores the unintended consequences of our individual actions for women as a class (and for other oppressed groups). *If you don't think you should care about the content of your choice, then you don't have to care about how that choice affects others.*

As I pointed out in the first chapter, I, like members of Renewal, was reluctant to acknowledge that inequalities existed there. Seeking a home away from the conventional sociology department and the uncomfortable role of "professing," I was invested in seeing an alternative organization and its members as virtuous. I had to analyze my investment in that belief in order to write the story.

Although I did not use the terms "false consciousness" and "internalized sexism" in the book I wrote about Renewal, my analysis made use of them. "False consciousness" is as out of fashion as "victim." It seems to insult those we study; participants may *think* they're doing the right thing, but *we* know better. Yet only by giving credence to the existence of gender inequality and the women's acceptance of it did I become able to develop empathy for the women on staff. By writing a critical appreciation, I gave the women credit for their efforts and ideals, but also examined how they unwittingly played a part in reinforcing their subordinate position. By looking closely at the contradictions between participants' ideals and their behaviors, and especially at the women's lack of awareness of practitioners' privileges, I could ask: How do people in a subordinate group manage to normalize their own subordination?

When participants resist the status quo, feminist fieldworkers probably have no difficulty saying that those we study are exercising agency. As I learned through my study of Renewal, however, not seeing inequality *also* entails agency. Once I conducted in-depth interviews with the staff women, I learned how they came to participate at Renewal, what they got out of being there, and how it wasn't (yet) in their interest to develop a quasi-sociological understanding of their position within it. As Jean Grimshaw (1986) wrote:

> I believe it is wrong to present a conception of woman *merely* as victim; nevertheless I think it is crucial to recognize the ways in which women are sometimes disabled and oppressed by the very qualities which are also in a way their strength. (p. 202)

False consciousness is not a label that serves as an explanation; it offers only a start for analysis. As feminist fieldworkers, we can then ask: What do those in the subordinate group want? What do they gain, individually, from their beliefs, even if those beliefs also reinforce their subordination as a class? And, if false consciousness changes over time, we can examine how those changes came about. My denial of inequalities suppressed those questions. A shift in feminist consciousness brought them to the fore.

And what about the powerful? Feminists are, understandably, much less worried about lacking empathy for those who have a lot of privilege. But just as false consciousness does not imply that members of a subordinate group are cultural dopes (Garfinkel, 1965), we need not assume that members of the powerful group are diabolical. Many inequalities persist because people keep doing business as usual, or, as Johnson (2005) put it, taking the path of least resistance. At Renewal, the male practitioners carried the authority of being men into an alternative organization. They didn't expect extra points just because they were white, straight, romantically available, middle-class, alternative professionals. Nor did they consciously put the staff women in the position of organizational housewives. But cultural beliefs, practices, and power relationships from the surrounding field—the larger society—informed what went on at Renewal, even as participants tried to develop an alternative. As feminist fieldworkers, we need to think about the larger context and how it shapes local realities.

As I have said in my classes, we cannot make progressive change if we are unwilling to look at systematic patterns of inequality, including those we are invested in. As Frye (1992) wrote:

> Naming patterns is like charting prevailing winds over a continent; there is no implication that every individual and item in the landscape is identically affected. For instance, male violence patterns experiences as different as that of overprotective paternalism and of incest, as different as the veil and the bikini. (p. 66)

Frye's reference to the bikini and the veil directs us to look below the surface as we engage in feminist analysis. What first look like opposite phenomena may in fact be part of the same larger pattern. For example, instead of thinking of the veil as indicative of oppression and the bikini as indicative of liberation (or "permissiveness"), we can think about what they might have in common.

In addition, there are contexts in which participants' practices will be intended as resistance, but end up reinforcing rather than reducing oppression. Participants' intentions and practices, and the consequences of participants' desires and actions, provide the empirical pieces of a feminist analysis.

By telling us how people reproduce inequalities, feminist analyses give us ideas about how to interrupt or undo that reproduction. As Nancy Hartsock (1998) wrote, "Feminism as a mode of analysis relies on the idea that we come to know the world, to change it, and be changed by it, through our everyday activity" (p. 36). How can we use the knowledge gained from feminist analyses—and the principles underlying them—to work on making change?

One possibility is by giving feedback to the organization or group we've studied to let them know how their organizational arrangements or cultural understandings reinforce inequalities. I was unable to test out participants' reactions to my study of Renewal because the organization no longer existed and members had dispersed. But looking back, I think it's unlikely that members of the dominant group (the male practitioners) would have accepted the analysis. Because the staff women developed a quasi-sociological analysis and eventually left the organization, they probably would have been receptive to much of what I wrote.

Nevertheless, a sociological critique might have struck many of the participants as limited at best and, at worst, superficial, cold, or unfair. Participants' "processing" at retreats denied power relations between groups; they reduced conflicts to "psychological dynamics" and "personal issues." Although dominants can act out of group interest without knowing it, I doubt the practitioners would have felt assuaged by words like "unwittingly" or "unintentionally." So it's possible that sharing findings with participants will affirm our analysis rather than motivate members to make changes in their organization. Knowing participants' language and how they think might help us translate our analysis into words that could reduce defensiveness. But there's no guarantee. As at Renewal, people who are invested in a moral identity might not want to hear that their behavior isn't matching their claims.

Then again, we might be surprised. Kolb (personal communication, 2000), who studied the black campus organization I discussed in Chapter 4, had a long dinner with female participants near the end of his study. He discussed his findings with them, including the pattern of women privileging the few men who joined the group (even after the men made consequential mistakes). Kolb had participated in the group's activism during his fieldwork and spent a lot of time with key participants. But as a white man telling black women that they were reinforcing sexism by putting the black men center stage, he did not expect the women to welcome his remarks. As it turned out, the women appreciated his analysis; by the end of the meal, they had provided him with more examples to support his analysis.

Getting feedback from participants also gives us the opportunity to find out if we have misperceived what went on. Participants' reactions provide data and could deepen the analysis. In the end, however, the analytic story remains ours alone. As Gorelick (1989) put it, "I will have the last word, and their [the respondents'] participation, including their disagreements with my interpretation, will end up, willy nilly, being grist for my mill" (p. 352). Even if we are doing participatory action research, we might discover that our answers to participants' questions about how to resolve their problems are not the ones they want to hear. As one group of researchers discovered, members of the organization they studied did not want to make gender equity a central concern, despite an initial interest in it (Ely & Meyerson, 2000; Meyerson & Kolb, 2000). The researchers' critique asked members to "hold open to scrutiny . . . the most fundamental aspects of the organization . . . to question the ways they themselves [had] become successful . . . [to challenge] the very way they live[d] their lives" (Ely & Meyerson, 2000, p. 600).

And what about our own lives? Will we find ways to apply our feminist insights and analyses to the groups, organizations, and institutions of which we are a part? If we take seriously the idea that whatever we study does not stand alone but is a case of something larger (Becker, 1998, pp. 125–128), then we should be able to generalize our knowledge to other settings. I did not expect the study of a holistic health center to lead me to analyze and challenge various organizations before I wrote *Opposing Ambitions* (Kleinman, 1996). But that analysis sensitized me to other places in which people who value solidarity and inclusiveness use those rhetorics in ways that maintain inequalities.

For example, I asked a local rape crisis center to be a cosponsor of the March to Save Women's Lives (initially called the March for Choice) in April 2004. Being listed on the Web site was the only requirement for cosponsorship; more than 1,000 organizations had signed on before I made my request. A majority of the board members voted against cosponsorship, arguing that taking such a stance might be unappealing to some of their clients and thus would not be "inclusive." Around the same time, some of us serving on the board of a university women's center suggested that the director add a list of 10 goals to the center's Web site, including "Maintaining and improving reproductive rights for all women." A few board members and administrators argued against doing so, saying that not all women at the university were pro-choice and that the center is supposed to represent "all women."

Although no one articulated this position, some board members and administrators (at both sites) probably worried about alienating donors and didn't want to admit it. But I was struck by the positive-sounding language (inclusiveness, representing all women) they used to opt out of taking a stance in favor of women's self-determination and moral autonomy. Those of us who argued with board members and administrators responded to their language, arguing that while a center should offer its *services* to all women, it does not have to represent the *views* of all women. (Would they want to represent the views of racist or heterosexist women, we asked?) We pointed out that "inclusiveness" is an impossible goal and would prevent an organization from taking a strong stand on anything. An "all-inclusive" policy in this case, we said, would subvert the organization's reason for being: empowering women.

Several of us spoke at a board meeting of the rape crisis center, addressing their concerns, and they took a second vote. We won over a few more members, but we lost the vote. At the women's center we managed to improve the mission statement that appears on the Web site, but administrators did not accept our list of goals.

We had other kinds of success. Members of progressive student groups who volunteered or worked at the centers learned firsthand about the potential dangers of the language of "representing both sides" (for instance, having a program on reproductive rights that would include a pro-choice and an anti-choice speaker) and "inclusiveness." They wrote letters to both centers (and in the case of the university, high-level administrators) expressing their dismay. The progressive students resigned from the programming committee of the campus women's center (they had been working steadily on producing a week of events, put on yearly by the center). The students, along with some faculty and community members, created a parallel week of events. After being informed about what had transpired, the keynote speakers for the women's center program agreed to speak at the "alternative" program. The media picked up on the story, and the free publicity they provided probably accounted in part for the high attendance at the events.

Looking back, our main success could be called educational. Students learned, firsthand, about the potential harm of "nice" language. They also learned that women can reinforce inequality (most of the board members and at least one key administrator were women), and that not taking a stand (for instance, remaining "neutral" about abortion) enables the continued erosion of reproductive rights.

Most of us who do feminist fieldwork are also in the "business" of education, so we have opportunities to bring feminist analyses to students who can then apply them. The studies discussed in *Feminist Fieldwork Analysis* can be used in undergraduate and graduate classes on inequality to highlight and illustrate feminist principles. Students find fieldwork studies compelling because they offer people's words, actions, and a story that sticks (see Kleinman, 1997). For instance, female students become surprised and angry to hear that men will be riding the glass escalator in nursing and teaching, while hardworking women in blue-collar jobs will be harassed by their co-workers and supervisors, and even successful executive women might find themselves shipped to a program for "Bully Broads." Students who have read these tales have no trouble remembering the concept of "false parallels" or applying it to their lives. The same is true for other studies and other feminist principles.

Students often report that feminist classes are life changing (Kleinman, Copp, & Sandstrom, 2006). They take the principles and findings to other classes, relationships, workplaces, and campus groups. We too can spread feminist knowledge through informal interactions and official roles (professor, adviser for a student activist group, speaker on a panel, etc.). And we can write op-eds, letters to the editor, and essays for popular media that rely on what we have learned as feminist fieldworkers. This practice of public sociology (Burawoy, 2005) may go beyond formal communication.

With feminist principles as our backbone, we may find ourselves, like some of our students, practicing 24/7.

Feminist analysis does more than provide answers to empirical questions. Feminism has a moral basis—yes, an agenda—and we should claim it. If we think that sexism, heterosexism, racism, and class inequality are harmful, then our studies will aim to create knowledge useful for eradicating them. This position implies that not all individual choices—of what to study or how to live our lives—have equal value. Choices that reproduce domination and exploitation are a problem. We should instead seek choices that challenge systems of oppression and privilege, and that enhance the dignity and humanity of all people. It's those choices that make us feminists.

REFERENCES

Apple, M. W. (1999). The absent presence of race in education reform. *Race, Ethnicity & Education, 2*(1), 9–16.

Arendell, T. (1992). The social self as gendered: A masculinist discourse on divorce. *Symbolic Interaction, 15*(2), 151–181.

Arendell, T. (1997). Reflections on the researcher-researched relationship: A woman interviewing men. *Qualitative Sociology, 20*(3), 341–368.

Banerjee, N. (2001, August 10). Some bullies seek ways to soften up: Toughness has risks for women executives. *The New York Times*, p. C1.

Barber, A. M. (1995). *Business as usual: Maintaining inequality in a women's advocacy organization*. Unpublished master's thesis, University of North Carolina at Chapel Hill.

Bartky, S. L. (1991). *Femininity and domination*. New York: Routledge.

Barton, B. (2002). Dancing on the möbius strip: Challenging the sex war paradigm. *Gender & Society, 16*(5), 585–602.

Baumgardner, J., & Richards, A. (2003). The number one question about feminism. *Feminist Studies, 29*(2), 448–452.

Becker, H. S. (1998). *Tricks of the trade: How to think about your research while you're doing it*. Chicago: University of Chicago Press.

Bennett, J. (1989). Feminism and history. *Gender & History, 1*(3), 251–272.

Bennett, J. (2006). *History matters: Patriarchy and the challenge of feminism*. Philadelphia: University of Pennsylvania Press.

Bettie, J. (2003). *Women without class: Girls, race, and identity*. Berkeley: University of California Press.

Blumer, H. (1969). *Symbolic interactionism: Perspective and method*. Englewood Cliffs, NJ: Prentice Hall.

Bonilla-Silva, E. (2003). *Racism without racists: Color-blind racism and the persistence of racial inequality in the United States*. Lanham, MD: Rowman & Littlefield.

Booth, K. M. (2004). *Local women, global science: Fighting AIDS in Kenya*. Bloomington: Indiana University Press.

Brines, J. (1994). Economic dependency, gender, and the division of labor at home. *American Journal of Sociology, 100*(3), 652–688.

Brown, E. (1993). *A taste of power: A black woman's story*. New York: Anchor Books.

Burawoy, M. (2005). For public sociology. *American Sociological Review, 70*(1), 4–28.

Cahill, S. (1999). Emotional capital and professional socialization: The case of mortuary science students (and me). *Social Psychology Quarterly, 62*(2), 101–116.

Cancian, F. M. (1992). Feminist science: Methodologies that challenge inequality. *Gender & Society, 6*(4), 623–642.

Carbado, D. (1999). Epilogue: Straight out of the closet: Men, feminism, and heterosexual privilege. In D. Carbado (Ed.), *Black men on race, gender, and sexuality* (pp. 417–447). New York: New York University Press.

118

Catalana, S. M. (2005). *Bureau of Justice Statistics national criminal victimization survey; criminal victimization 2004* (NCJ Publication No. 210674). Retrieved July 21, 2006, from http://www.rainn.org/docs/statistics/ncvs2004.pdf

Cohn, C. (2000a). "How can she claim equal rights when she doesn't have to do as many push-ups as I do?": The framing of men's opposition to women's equality in the military. *Masculinities, 3*(2), 131–151.

Cohn, C. (2000b). Wars, wimps, and women: Talking gender and thinking war. In M. S. Kimmel & A. Aronson (Eds.), *The gendered society reader* (1st ed., pp. 362–374). New York: Oxford University Press.

Cole, J. B., & Guy-Sheftall, B. (2003). *Gender talk: The struggle for women's equality in African American communities.* New York: Ballantine.

Collins, P. H. (1990). *Black feminist thought.* New York: Routledge.

Connell, R. W. (1995). *Masculinities.* Berkeley: University of California Press.

Crenshaw, K. (1995). Mapping the margins: Intersectionality, identity politics, and violence against women of colour. In K. Crenshaw, N. Gotanda, G. Peller, & K. Thomas (Eds.), *Critical race theory: The key writings that formed the movement* (pp. 357–383). New York: New Press.

Curry, T. J. (1991). Fraternal bonding in the locker room: A profeminist analysis of talk about competition and women. *Sociology of Sport Journal, 8*(2), 119–135.

Davis, A. Y. (1981). *Women, race and class.* New York: Random House.

Deutsch, F. M. (2004). Strategies men use to resist. In M. S. Kimmel & M. A. Messner (Eds.), *Men's lives* (6th ed., pp. 469–475). Boston: Allyn & Bacon.

DeVault, M. L. (1999). *Liberating method: Feminism and social research.* Philadelphia: Temple University Press.

Dewey, J. (1984). The quest for certainty. In J. A. Boydston (Ed.), *John Dewey: The later works, 1925–1953: Vol. 4. 1929.* Carbondale, IL: Southern Illinois University Press. (Original work published 1929)

Diaz, R. M. (2004). Trips to fantasy island: Contexts of risky sex for San Francisco gay men. In M. S. Kimmel & M. A. Messner (Eds.), *Men's lives* (6th ed., pp. 363–379). Boston: Allyn & Bacon.

Dillon, S. (2005, January 18). Harvard chief defends his talk on women. *The New York Times,* p. A16, column 14.

Dunn, J. L. (2002). *Courting disaster: Intimate stalking, culture, and criminal justice.* New York: Aldine de Gruyter.

Ely, R. J., & Meyerson, D. E. (2000). Advancing gender equity in organizations: The challenge and importance of maintaining a gender narrative. *Organization, 7*(4), 589–608.

Emerson, R. M., Fretz, R. I., & Shaw, L. L. (1995). *Writing ethnographic fieldnotes.* Chicago: University of Chicago Press.

Esterberg, K. G. (2002). *Qualitative methods in social research.* New York: McGraw-Hill.

Ezzell, M. B. (2004). *"Kicking ass and looking good": Reinforcing sexism through women's rugby.* Unpublished master's thesis, University of North Carolina at Chapel Hill.

Ferguson, A. A. (2001). *Bad boys: Public schools in the making of black masculinity*. Ann Arbor: University of Michigan Press.

Fields, J. (2005). "Children having children": Race, innocence, and sexuality education. *Social Problems, 52*, 549–571.

Fields, J., Copp, M., & Kleinman, S. (2006). Symbolic interactionism, inequality, and emotions. In J. E. Stets & J. Turner (Eds.), *Handbook of the sociology of emotions* (pp. 155–178). New York: Springer.

Fine, M. (2006). Bearing witness: Methods for researching oppression and resistance—a textbook for critical research. *Social Justice Research, 19*(1), 83–108.

Fish, S. (1994). Reverse racism, or, how the pot got to call the kettle black. In *There's no such thing as free speech (and it's a good thing, too)* (pp. 60–69). New York: Oxford University Press.

Fonow, M. M., & Cook, J. A. (1991). *Beyond methodology: Feminist scholarship as lived research*. Bloomington: Indiana University Press.

Forer, A. (1978). Thoughts on consciousness-raising. In Redstockings (Ed.), *Feminist revolution: An abridged edition with additional writings* (p. 151). New York: Random House.

Frankenberg, R. (1993). *White women, race matters: The social construction of whiteness*. Minneapolis: University of Minnesota Press.

Frye, M. (1983). *The politics of reality: Essays in feminist theory*. Trumansburg, New York: Crossing Press.

Frye, M. (1992). *Willful virgin: Essays in feminism*. Trumansburg, NY: Crossing Press.

Garfinkel, H. (1965). *Studies in ethnomethodology*. Englewood Cliffs, NJ: Prentice Hall.

Gerschick, T. J., & Miller, A. S. (1994). Gender identities at the crossroads of masculinity and disability. *Masculinities, 2*, 34–55.

Gilligan, C. (1982). *In a different voice: Psychological theory and women's development*. Cambridge, MA: Harvard University Press.

Giuffre, P. A., & Williams, C. L. (1994). Boundary lines: Labeling sexual harassment in restaurants. *Gender & Society, 8*(3), 378–401.

Goffman, E. (1959). *The presentation of self in everyday life*. Garden City, NY: Doubleday.

Gorelick, S. (1989). The changer and the changed: Methodological reflections on studying Jewish feminists. In A. M. Jaggar & S. R. Bordo (Eds.), *Gender/body/knowledge: Feminist reconstructions of being and knowing* (pp. 336–358). New Brunswick, NJ: Rutgers University Press.

Grimshaw, J. (1986). *Philosophy and feminist thinking*. Minneapolis: University of Minnesota Press.

Hanisch, C. (2006). The personal is political. Retrieved July 24, 2006, from http://scholar.alexanderstreet.com/download/attachments/2259/Personal+Is+Pol.pdf?version=1

Harding, S. (1987). *Feminism and methodology: Social science issues*. Bloomington: Indiana University Press.

Harding, S. (1993). Rethinking standpoint theory: "What is strong objectivity?" In L. Alcoff & E. Potter (Eds.), *Feminist epistemologies* (pp. 49–82). New York: Routledge.

Harding, S. (2004). *The feminist standpoint theory reader: Intellectual and political controversies.* New York: Routledge.

Hartmann, H., Gault, B., & Williams, E. (2005). Memo to John Roberts: The gender wage gap is real (IWPR Publication No. C362). Retrieved July 22, 2006, from http://www.iwpr.org/pdf/C362.pdf

Hartsock, N. C. M. (1998). *The feminist standpoint revisited and other essays.* Boulder, CO: Westview Press.

Harvey, J. (1999). *Civilized oppression.* Lanham, MD: Rowman & Littlefield.

Hawkesworth, M. E. (2006). *Feminist inquiry: From political conviction to methodological innovation.* New Brunswick, NJ: Rutgers University Press.

Heath, M. (2003). Soft-boiled masculinity: Renegotiating gender and racial ideologies in the Promise Keepers movement. *Gender & Society, 17*(3), 423–444.

Henson, K. D., & Rogers, J. K. (2001). "Why Marcia you've changed!" Male clerical temporary workers doing masculinity in a feminized occupation. *Gender & Society, 15*(2), 218–238.

Higgenbotham, E. B. (1993). *Righteous discontent: The women's movement in the black Baptist church, 1880–1920.* Cambridge, MA: Harvard University Press.

Hochschild, A. R. (1983). *The managed heart: Commercialization of human feeling.* Berkeley: University of California Press.

Hochschild, A. R. (1989a). The economy of gratitude. In D. D. Franks & E. D. McCarthy (Eds.), *The sociology of emotions: Original essays and research papers* (pp. 95–113). Greenwich, CT: JAI Press.

Hochschild, A. R. (1989b). *The second shift: Working parents and the revolution at home.* New York: Viking Press.

Hofstadter, D. R. (1985). A person paper on purity in language. In *Metamagical themas: Questing for the essence of mind and pattern* (pp. 159–172). New York: Basic Books.

Hondagneu-Sotelo, P. (2001). *Doméstica: Immigrant workers cleaning and caring in the shadows of affluence.* Berkeley: University of California Press.

hooks, b. (1989). *Talking back: Thinking feminist, thinking black.* Boston: South End Press.

hooks, b. (1990). Critical interrogation: Talking race, resisting racism. In b. hooks (Ed.), *Yearning: Race, gender, and cultural politics* (pp. 51–55). Boston: South End Press.

Jackall, R. (1988). *Moral mazes: The world of corporate managers.* New York: Oxford University Press.

Jaggar, A. M. (1989). Love and knowledge: Emotion in feminist epistemology. In A. M. Jaggar & S. R. Bordo (Eds.), *Gender/body/knowledge: Feminist reconstructions of being and knowing* (pp. 145–171). New Brunswick, NJ: Rutgers University Press.

James, W. (2000). *Pragmatism and other writings*. New York: Penguin Books.

Johnson, A. G. (2005). *The gender knot: Unraveling our patriarchal legacy* (Rev. ed.). Philadelphia: Temple University Press.

Kanter, R. M. (1977). *Men and women of the corporation*. New York: Basic Books.

Katz, J. (2006). *The macho paradox: Why some men hurt women and how all men can help*. Naperville, IL: Sourcebooks.

Katz, J., & Jhally, S. (1999, May 2). The national conversation in the wake of Littleton is missing the mark. *The Boston Globe*, p. E1.

Kleinman, S. (1996). *Opposing ambitions: Gender and identity in an alternative organization*. Chicago: University of Chicago Press.

Kleinman, S. (1997). Essaying the personal: Making sociological stories stick. *Qualitative Sociology, 20*(4), 553–564.

Kleinman, S. (1998). What sociology teaches me. *Sociological Analysis, 1*(2), 119–124.

Kleinman, S. (2002a). Emotions, fieldwork, and professional lives. In T. May (Ed.), *Qualitative research in action* (pp. 375–394). London: Sage.

Kleinman, S. (2002b). Why sexist language matters. *Qualitative Sociology, 25*(2), 299–304.

Kleinman, S. (2003). Feminist fieldworker: Connecting research, teaching, and memoir. In B. Glassner & R. Hertz (Eds.), *Our studies, ourselves* (pp. 215–232). New York: Oxford University Press.

Kleinman, S., & Copp, M. A. (1993). *Emotions and fieldwork*. Newbury Park, CA: Sage.

Kleinman, S., Copp, M., & Sandstrom, K. (2006). Making sexism visible: Birdcages, Martians, and pregnant men. *Teaching Sociology, 24*(2), 126–142.

Kolb, K. H. (2000). *"Supporting our black men": Reproducing male privilege among black student activists*. Unpublished master's thesis, University of North Carolina at Chapel Hill.

Krauss, C. (1993). Women and toxic waste protests: Race, class, and gender as resources of resistance. *Qualitative Sociology, 16*(3), 247–262.

Lakoff, R. T. (1975). *Language and women's place*. New York: Harper & Row.

Lareau, A. (2003). *Unequal childhoods: Class, race, and family life*. Berkeley: University of California Press.

Lofland, J., Snow, D., Anderson, L., & Lofland, L. (2005). *Analyzing social settings: A guide to qualitative observation and analysis* (4th ed.). Belmont, CA: Wadsworth.

Lorber, J. (2004). "Night to his day": The social construction of gender. In L. Richardson, V. Taylor, & N. Whittier (Eds.), *Feminist frontiers* (6th ed., pp. 33–51). New York: McGraw-Hill.

Lorber, J. (2005). *Breaking the bowls: Degendering and feminist change*. New York: W. W. Norton.

Martin, P. Y. (2003). "Said and done" versus "saying and doing": Gender practices, practicing gender at work. *Gender & Society, 17*(3), 342–366.

Martin, P. Y., & Hummer, R. A. (1989). Fraternities and rape on campus. *Gender & Society, 3*(4), 457–473.

122

McMahon, M. (1995). *Engendering motherhood: Identity and self-transformation in women's lives*. New York: Guilford Press.

McQueeney, K. (2006). *"Who I am in God and who God is in me": Race, class, gender, and sexuality in lesbian- and gay-affirming Protestant congregations*. Unpublished doctoral dissertation, University of North Carolina at Chapel Hill.

Mead, G. H. (1934). *Mind, self & society from the standpoint of a social behaviorist*. Chicago: University of Chicago Press.

Mead, G. H. (1938). *The philosophy of the act*. Chicago: University of Chicago Press.

Messner, M. (1989). Masculinities and athletic careers. *Gender & Society, 3*(1), 71–88.

Messner, M. A. (1993). "Changing Men" and feminist politics in the United States. *Theory and Society, 22*(5), 723–737.

Meyerson, D. E., & Kolb, D. M. (2000). Moving out of the "armchair": Developing a framework to bridge the gap between feminist theory and practice. *Organization, 7*(4), 553–571.

Miller, J. B. (1976). *Toward a new psychology of women*. Boston: Beacon Press.

Mills, T., & Kleinman, S. (1988). Emotions, reflexivity, and action: An interactionist analysis. *Social Forces, 66*(4), 1009–1027.

Murphy, E. F., & Graff, E. J. (2005). *Getting even: Why women don't get paid like men—and what to do about it*. New York: Simon & Schuster.

Naples, N. A. (2003). *Feminism and method: Ethnography, discourse analysis, and activist research*. New York: Routledge.

Oliker, S. J. (1989). *Best friends and marriage: Exchange among women*. Berkeley: University of California Press.

Ottenberg, S. (1990). Thirty years of fieldnotes: Changing relationships to the text. In R. Sanjek (Ed.), *Fieldnotes: The makings of anthropology* (pp. 139–160). Ithaca: Cornell University Press.

Padavic, I. (1991). The re-creation of gender in a male workplace. *Symbolic Interaction, 14*(3), 279–294.

Parker, G. M. (1997). *Trespassing: My sojourn in the halls of privilege*. Boston: Houghton Mifflin.

Parreñas, R. S. (2001). *Servants of globalization: Women, migration and domestic work*. Palo Alto: Stanford University Press.

Pharr, S. (1997). *Homophobia: A weapon of sexism*. Berkeley, CA: Chardon Press.

Phillips, S. P., & Schneider, M. S. (1993). Sexual harassment of female doctors by patients. *New England Journal of Medicine, 329,* 1936–1939.

Pierce, J. L. (1995). *Gender trials: Emotional lives in contemporary law*. Berkeley: University of California Press.

Ramazanoglu, C. (with Holland, J.). (2002). *Feminist methodology: Challenges and choices*. Thousand Oaks, CA: Sage.

Reskin, B. F. (1988). Bringing the men back in: Sex differentiation and the devaluation of women's work. *Gender & Society, 2*(1), 58–81.

Rhode, D. L. (1997). *Speaking of sex: The denial of gender inequality*. Cambridge, MA: Harvard University Press.

Richardson, L. (2004). Gender stereotyping in the English language. In L. Richardson, V. Taylor, & N. Whittier (Eds.), *Feminist frontiers* (6th ed., pp. 89–93). New York: McGraw-Hill.

Roberts, D. (1997). *Killing the black body: Race, reproduction, and the meaning of liberty.* New York: Pantheon Books.

Rollins, J. (1986). *Between women: Domestics and their employers.* Philadelphia: Temple University Press.

Romero, M. (1992). *Maid in the U.S.A.* New York: Routledge.

Rothenberg, B. (2003). "We don't have time for social change": Cultural compromise and the battered woman syndrome. *Gender & Society, 17*(5), 771–787.

Rothschild, J., & Whitt, J. A. (1986). *The cooperative workplace: Potentials and dilemmas of organizational democracy and participation.* New York: Cambridge University Press.

Rubin, L. B. (1983). *Intimate strangers: Men and women together* (1st ed.). New York: Harper & Row.

Russo, A. (2001). *Taking back our lives: A call to action for the feminist movement.* New York: Routledge.

Sabo, D. (2004). Masculinities and men's health: Moving toward post-superman era prevention. In M. S. Kimmel & M. A. Messner (Eds.), *Men's lives* (6th ed., pp. 321–334). Boston: Allyn & Bacon.

Sattel, J. (1976). The inexpressive male: Tragedy or sexual politics? *Social Problems, 23,* 469–477.

Schwalbe, M. (1996). *Unlocking the iron cage: The men's movement, gender politics, and American culture.* New York: Oxford University Press.

Schwalbe, M. (2000). The elements of inequality. *Contemporary Sociology, 29*(6), 775–781.

Schwalbe, M. (2005). *The sociologically examined life: Pieces of the conversation* (3rd ed.). New York: McGraw-Hill.

Schwalbe, M., Godwin, S., Holden, D., Schrock, D., Thompson, S., & Wolkomir, M. (2000). Generic processes in the reproduction of inequality: An interactionist analysis. *Social Forces, 79*(2), 419–452.

Scott, M. B., & Lyman, S. M. (1968). Accounts. *American Sociological Review, 33*(1), 46–62.

Scully, D., & Marolla, J. (1990). Convicted rapists' vocabulary of motive: Excuses and justifications. In D. Brissett & C. Edgeley (Eds.), *Life as theater: A dramaturgical source book* (pp. 261–280). New York: Aldine de Gruyter.

Seager, J. (1993). *Earth follies: Coming to feminist terms with the global environmental crisis.* New York: Routledge.

Silliman, J., Fried, M. G., Ross, L., & Gutierrez, E. (2004). *Undivided rights: Women of color organize for reproductive justice* (1st ed.). Cambridge, MA: South End Press.

Smith, D. (1990). *The conceptual practices of power: A feminist sociology of knowledge.* Boston: Northeastern University Press.

Solinger, R. (2000). *Wake up little Susie: Single pregnancy and race before Roe v. Wade.* New York: Routledge.

Spender, D. (1985). *Man made language* (2nd ed.). New York: Routledge.

Sprague, J. (2005). *Feminist methodologies for critical researchers: Bridging differences.* Walnut Creek, CA: AltaMira Press.

Stenross, B., & Kleinman, S. (1989). The highs and lows of emotional labor: Detectives' encounters with criminals and victims. *Journal of Contemporary Ethnography, 17*(4), 435–452.

Summers, L. H. (2005). *Remarks at NBER conference on diversifying the science & engineering workforce.* Retrieved July 24, 2006, from http://www.president. harvard.edu/speeches/2005/nber.html

Tallichet, S. E. (1995). Gendered relations in the mines and the division of labor underground. *Gender & Society, 9*(6), 697–711.

Thomas, J. (1993). *Doing critical ethnography.* Newbury Park, CA: Sage.

Thompson, B. W. (2004). "A way outta no way": Eating problems among African-American, Latina, and white women. In L. Richardson, V. Taylor, & N. Whittier (Eds.), *Feminist frontiers* (6th ed., pp. 353–363). New York: McGraw-Hill.

Tichenor, V. J. (2005). *Earning more and getting less: Why successful wives can't buy equality.* New Brunswick, NJ: Rutgers University Press.

Tolar, L. (2001, September 4). Sexism's latest form. *The News and Observer,* p. A10.

Tolman, D. L. (2002). *Dilemmas of desire: Teenage girls talk about sexuality.* Cambridge, MA: Harvard University Press.

Turner, R. H. (1976). The real self: From institution to impulse. *American Journal of Sociology, 81*(5), 989–1016.

United States Census Bureau. (n.d.). *Selected characteristics of people, by total money income in 2004, work experience in 2004, race, Hispanic origin, and sex.* Retrieved July 22, 2006, from http://pubdb3.census.gov/macro/032005/perinc/ new01_000.htm

Walby, S. (1990). *Theorizing patriarchy.* Cambridge, MA: Blackwell.

Wellman, D. T. (1993). *Portraits of white racism* (2nd ed.). New York: Cambridge University Press.

West, C. (1992). When the doctor is a "lady": Power, status, and gender in physician-patient encounters. In H. A. Farberman, G. A. Fine, & J. Johnson (Eds.), *Social psychological foundations: Readings from an interactionist perspective* (pp. 287–306). Greenwich, CT: JAI Press.

West, C., & Fenstermaker, S. (1995). Doing difference. *Gender & Society, 9*(1), 8–37.

West, C., & Zimmerman, D. H. (1987). Doing gender. *Gender & Society, 1*(2), 125–151.

White, E. F. (2001). *Dark continent of our bodies: Black feminism and the politics of respectability.* Philadelphia: Temple University Press.

Wilkins, A. C. (2004a). Puerto Rican wannabes: Sexual spectacle and the marking of race, class, and gender boundaries. *Gender & Society, 18*(1), 103–121.

Wilkins, A. C. (2004b). "So full of myself as a chick": Goth women, sexual independence, and gender egalitarianism. *Gender & Society, 18*(3), 328–349.

Wilkins, A. C. (in press). *Wannabes, Goths, and Christians: Gender, race, class, and sexuality in youth cultures.* Chicago: University of Chicago Press.

Williams, C. L. (1995). *Still a man's world: Men who do "women's" work.* Berkeley: University of California Press.

Wolkomir, M. (2004). "Giving it up to God": Negotiating femininity in support groups for wives of ex-gay Christian men. *Gender & Society, 18*(6), 735–755.

Wolkomir, M. (2006). *"Be not deceived": The sacred and sexual struggles of gay and ex-gay Christian men.* New Brunswick, NJ: Rutgers University Press.

Zelizer, V. A. (1989). The social meaning of money: "Special monies." *American Journal of Sociology, 95*(2), 342–377.

INDEX

ABOUT THE AUTHOR

Sherryl Kleinman is Professor of Sociology at the University of North Carolina at Chapel Hill. She is author of *Equals Before God: Seminarians as Humanistic Professionals* (1984) and *Opposing Ambitions: Gender and Identity in an Alternative Organization* (1996) and coauthor, with Martha Copp, of *Emotions and Fieldwork* (1993). In addition to doing academic work in the areas of symbolic interaction, fieldwork, sociology of emotions, and inequality, she has published poetry and creative nonfiction in magazines, literary journals, and newspapers.

Qualitative Research Methods

Series Editor
JOHN VAN MAANEN
Massachusetts Institute of Technology

Associate Editors:
Peter K. Manning, *Northeastern University*
& Marc L. Miller, *University of Washington*